PRAYING
through the
PROMISES
of
GOD

Archbishop N. Duncan-Williams

CONTENTS

Personal Word

I have been in the ministry of our LORD Jesus Christ over twenty years, and one of the strong, God-given weapons that has kept me standing after fierce attacks and counter attacks by the forces of hell has been prayer. At certain points in my life when there seemed to be no way out of difficult and seemingly impossible situations, strong prayer offered up to God caused there to be a miraculous turnaround in my circumstances.

Over the last few years, I have been extremely burdened by the apathetic and lazy attitude with which most Christians treat prayer. The enemy has managed to deceive countless multitudes of God's children into thinking there is no need for prayer in their lives. They have been deceived by the forces of darkness to turn away from the one thing that carries the capability to deliver them from the challenges which confront and oppose them in their walk with God.

In the realm of the spirit, I looked and saw strategic and well-organized battle positioning of the enemy designed to blot out prayer from the church of our LORD Jesus Christ. To some measure the enemy has succeeded, because the church has allowed this by yielding to his deceptive tactics.

In September 1994, I was in America when the Holy Ghost spoke to me and told me to write a series called, "It Is Time to Pray." He said, "I am going to use this book to turn the prayer lives of millions of my people around." *Birthing the Promises of God in Travail* is the first book of the series.

It is my prayer that as you read this book, the Holy Ghost will cause the blindness and deception over your spiritual eyes to be lifted, and that there shall come a supernatural quickening of your spirit man to stand tall and become a battle axe in the hand of the Almighty God in the realm of spiritual warfare. It is also my prayer that not only will your prayer life change dramatically, but that you will pray so fervently that there will be miraculous and supernatural changes in your personal life, that of your family, and your local church.

I urge you to read this book prayerfully. Remember you are receiving information the enemy does not want you to have. An enemy exposed is a dangerous foe. No doubt he will attempt to throw you off this path by intimidation or an out-right attack. I urge you to keep yourself covered with prayer as you move forward in this new knowledge, holding fast to God's promise that we are more than conquerors through Christ Jesus.

In this end time, it is those with the capacity to break the power of hell that will move forward and achieve the deep purposes of God concerning their lives. You now have a God-given opportunity; take it and run.

Yours for the demolition of strongholds,

Archbishop Nicholas Duncan-Williams

Introduction

From the stand point of prophetic prayer, one of the most crucial Scriptures in the entire Bible is the following:

> *This charge I commit unto thee, son Timothy, according to the prophecies which went before on thee, that thou by them mightest war a good warfare; Holding faith, and a good conscience; which some having put away concerning faith have made shipwreck:*   *1 Timothy 1:18-19*

By this charge, Paul gave Timothy the keys whereby he would be able to secure the purposes of God concerning his life and would not end up shipwrecked in the great spiritual battle raging in the heavenlies and on earth. Paul also made it clear that the manifestation of God's promises and prophecies would be brought about by warfare.

In my many years in ministry, I have come to notice an extremely effective deception from the forces of darkness against Christians. Christians have assumed that as long as God has given a promise of prophecy it will come to pass. "So let us just relax, sleep, and wait for it to be fulfilled." I repeat, this attitude is a result of a great deception from the forces of hell.

How many times has a powerful prophecy of what God intends to do concerning an individual, family, or church has been given through the Holy Ghost, only to be followed shortly after with things going from bad to worse, teetering on the brink of collapse? Notice how many times a prophecy comes over an individual that God is going to do something special in his or her life—and then the opposite happens. In light of these turn of events, observers stand around wondering whether the prophecy was true in the first place.

Let me establish one important fact. Satan and his forces do not know the exact purposes of God concerning you in a particular area until the purposes are revealed by prophecy. Immediately after they discover a revelation, they take measures in the realm of the spirit and the natural to ensure that the prophecy never comes to pass. If a Christian decides to fold his arms and say, "because God said it, it shall surely come to pass," without praying it into manifestation, his prophecy can be aborted by the forces of darkness.

In Paul's letter to Timothy, Paul was effectively saying, "I am aware that you have a great call of God upon your life because of the prophetic utterances that have been spoken over you. But, these revealed purposes of God will not come to pass except you contend with the forces of darkness that seek to oppose and defeat them in the realm of the spirit."

A common error of believers is that they go rejoicing, dancing, *and then sleeping* when they receive a prophecy from the Lord. They believe that somehow the prophecy will come to pass automatically. It is the most dangerous route to take because the believer is now on Satan's hit list. As far as Satan is concerned, God has openly declared His intentions concerning His child in a particular area, and he (Satan) is not going to sit down and watch that prophecy come to pass. So he launches an all-out onslaught against the believer to crush and obliterate him from the face of the earth.

• A sad situation arises when the devil declares total war on a Christian, and he or she is not even aware of it. All sorts of things begin to go wrong.

And, the believer, under pressure, starts to question God: "Was it not God who said this or that was going to happen in my life? Why is the opposite happening?"

> *Therefore my people are gone into captivity, because they have no knowledge.*
> *Isaiah 5:13*

> *Lest Satan should get an advantage of us: for we are not ignorant of his devices.*
> *2 Corinthians 2:11*

The devil is happy when he comes into contact with an ignorant believer. Satan draws circles around such a one because he or she does not understand the principles of the kingdom and the rules of engagement in the realm of the spirit. Dear Reader, you may be thinking, "But, I have not received any spoken prophecy from the Lord over my life as Timothy or others have." Let this sink down deep into your spirit: the Bible is full of thousands of God's promises waiting to be manifested in the lives of believers. Most of God's promises do not come to pass because believers do not want to pay the price in prayer to effect their manifestation.

We face the deception that says, "Jesus died on the cross for me, so the promises of God in the Bible will somehow come to pass in my life." Let me stress this point, the promises of God revealed in His word for His people **are manifested through prayer**. We have to pray the promises into manifestation. There is no magic formula. We have to get on our knees and travail until we see the manifestation of what God said concerning us. There is no easy way out. **You either pray or you fail.**

... for as soon as Zion travailed, she brought forth her children.   Isaiah 66:8

In the next few chapters, we will look at the real life experiences from the Bible showing how certain individuals and nations birthed the promises of God through travail. You will discover that, in each case, it was warfare that brought the victory. Brethren, in this crucial time of world history we cannot afford to be complacent. We have to pray, or we will fail.

Chapter One

Breaking out of Egypt

The Prophecy

In Genesis 15, God decided to cut a covenant with Abraham. When Abraham had finished preparing the animals and bird sacrifices for the covenant, a strange thing happened.

And when the fowls came down upon the carcasses, Abram drove them away. And when the sun was going down a deep sleep fell upon Abram; and lo, an horror of great darkness fell upon him. And he said unto Abram, Know of a surety that thy seed shall be a stranger in a land that is not theirs, and shall serve them, and they shall afflict them four hundred years; And also that nation, whom they shall serve, will I judge: and afterward shall they come out with great substance. **Genesis 15:11-14**

Satan, being a student of prophecy, decided to frustrate God's purposes concerning His people. His ultimate plan was that, as soon as God's people entered into that land of bondage, he was going to ensure by every means at his disposal they would never come out. He therefore started to count the years immediately after Jacob—who was an heir to the promise, and a partaker of the covenant, and had passed through the borders of Egypt as a result of famine in Canaan. Genesis 46 gives us a glimpse of Jacob's crossing in Egypt:

All the souls that came with Jacob in Egypt, which came out of his loins, besides Jacob's sons' wives, all the souls were three-score and six;
And the sons of Joseph, which were born him in Egypt, were two souls: all the souls of the house of Jacob, which came into Egypt, were threescore and ten. **Genesis 46: 26-27**

Killing the Vision

From that point onward, Satan began counting the years. As the four hundred year mark drew near, he put his plans into action by influencing Pharaoh, the King of Egypt, to impose certain Draconian laws.

Now there arose up a new king over Egypt, which knew not Joseph.

And he said unto his people, Behold, the people of the children of Israel are more and mightier than we:

Come on, let us deal wisely with them; lest they multiply and it come to pass, that, when there falleth out any war, they join also unto our enemies, and fight against us, and so get them up out of the land.

Therefore they did set them taskmasters to afflict them with their burdens. And they built for Pharaoh treasure cities, Pithom and Raamses.

But the more they afflicted them, the more they multiplied and grew. And they were grieved because of the children of Israel.

And the Egyptians made the children of Israel to serve with rigor.

And they made their lives bitter with hard bondage, in mortar, and in brick, and in all manner of service in the field: all their service, wherein they made them serve, was with rigor.

And the king of Egypt spake to the Hebrew midwives, of which the name of one was, Shiphrah, and the name of the other Puah:

And he said, When ye do the office of a midwife to the Hebrew women, and see them upon the stools; if it be a son, then ye shall kill him: but if it be a daughter, then she shall live.

But the midwives feared God, and did not as the king of Egypt commanded them, but saved the men children alive.

And the king of Egypt called for the midwives, and said unto them, Why have ye done this thing, and have saved the men children alive?

And the midwives said unto Pharaoh, Because the Hebrew women are not as the Egyptian women; for they are lively, and are delivered ere the midwives come in unto them.

Therefore God dealt well with the midwives: and the people multiplied and waxed very mighty.

And it came to pass, because the midwives feared God, that he made them houses.

And Pharaoh charged all his people, saying, Every son that is born ye shall cast into the river, and every daughter ye shall save alive.   *Exodus 1:8-22*

*As far as Satan was concerned, he was taking no chances. The four hundred years of bondage was coming to an end, and he was prepared to go to every length to ensure that any deliver who God might use to lead His people out of bondage would be eliminated. Being an ex-archangel and, therefore an intelligent being, he knew that one of the unfailing principles of God was that deliverance would come through a man or a group pf people. Not knowing to which family the deliverer would be born, he decided not to take anything for granted. As a result, he influenced Pharaoh to make a demonically-inspired decree that every male child born to the Hebrews should be killed.

Many years later, he was to use a similar tactic in an effort to eliminate the infant Jesus when he influenced Herod the Great to pass an order that all male infants in Bethlehem and its surroundings area below the age of two years should be killed.

We see clearly from these two scenarios in Egypt, around the time of Moses' birth, and in Israel at the time of Christ's birth, that Satan greatly influenced the rulers of those nations to pass laws designed to combat and destroy the purposes of God.

May I suggest to you that things are not much different now than they were then. If anything at all, the situation now is worse. This generation is confronted with a web of demonically-inspired laws and legislations in more countries upon the face of the earth. These have been crafted to cripple Christians and reduce their activity into inactivity. They have also been designed to abort certain crucial prophecies in the Bible, which must, of a necessity, come to pass in this end time. If we as Christians are to really enter into the deep purposes of God concerning us, then we have to rise up in prayer and act as spiritual legislators to effect and enforce certain changes in the heavenlies. This rising up in prayer will bring about positive turnarounds in our families, churches, and nations.

Going back to Satan's machinations in Egypt and his determined effort to kill the deliverer, Jesus said, ***"The thief cometh not, but to steal, and to kill, and to destroy."*** (John 10:10).

In Egypt, Satan manifested his great ability to steal, to kill, and to destroy. It was under these conditions that Moses, the deliverer, was born. Stephen, as part of his defense to the council, gave an enlightened summary of what happened in those days.

♦ *But when the time of the promise drew nigh, which God had sworn to Abraham, the people grew and multiplied in Egypt,*

Till another king arose, which knew not Joseph.

The same dealt subtly with our kindred, and evil entreated our fathers, so that they cast out their young children, to the end they might not live.

In which time Moses was born, and was exceeding fair, and nourished up in his father's house three months:

And when he was cast out, Pharaoh's daughter took him up, and nourished him for her own son.

And Moses was learned in all the wisdom of the Egyptians, and was mighty in words and in deeds.

And when he was full forty years old, it came into his heart to visit his brethren the children of Israel.

And seeing one of them suffer wrong, he defended him, and avenged him that was oppressed, and smote the Egyptian:

For he supposed his brethren would have understood how that God by his hand would deliver them: but they understood not.

And the next day he showed himself unto them as they strove, and would have set them at one again, saying, Sirs, ye are brethren; why do ye wrong one to another?

But he that did his neighbor wrong thrust him away, saying, Who made thee a ruler and a judge over us?

Wilt thou kill me, as thou didst the Egyptian yesterday?

Then fled Moses at this saying, and was a stranger in the land of Madian, where he begat two sons.

And when forty years were expired, there appeared to him in the wilderness of Mount Sinai an angel of the Lord in a flame of fire in a bush.

When Moses saw it, he wondered at the sight: and as he drew near to behold it, the voice of the Lord came unto him,

Saying, I am the God of thy fathers, the God of Abraham, and the God of Isaac, and the God of Jacob. Then Moses trembled, and durst not behold.

Then said the Lord to him, Put off thy shoes from thy feet: for the place where thou standest is holy ground.

I have seen, I have seen the affliction of my people which is in Egypt, and I have heard their groaning, and am come down to deliver them. And now come, I will send thee into Egypt.

This Moses whom they refused, saying, Who made thee a ruler and a judge? The same did God send to be a ruler and a deliverer by the hand of the angel which appeared to him in the bush.

He brought them out, after that he had showed wonders and signs in the land of Egypt, and in the Red sea, and in the wilderness forty years.   *Acts 7:17-36*

It is important to realize that God did not commence His deliverance of the children of Israel in Egypt until prayer came up unto Him. The Bible account says that God heard their groaning and, as a result, came down to deliver them. If people had not cried out to God, nothing would have happened. Even though these were groans of despair and pain as a result of the hard bondage the people were serving under, they went up as a petition before God.

> *Who in the days of his flesh, when he had offered up prayers and supplications with strong crying and tears unto him that was able to save him from death, and was heard in that he feared.* **Hebrews 5:7**

• In the above Scripture and in Chapter Six of this book, you will come to understand that even Jesus, the Son of God, had to pray in order to stop Satan from interrupting the purposes of the Father concerning Him. How much more we, who were bought by His blood and transferred from Satan's kingdom into the kingdom of light, have to pray. We either have to pray or stare at failure. Remember, nothing happens until we cry, as the people in bondage in Egypt cried and their cries rose up to God.

The Judgment of Plagues

From the moment Moses appeared before Pharaoh, petitioning him to let the children of Israel go, the ruling Satanic forces over Egypt made a crucial decision—they were going to oppose this move and the purposes of God with every weapon in their arsenal. As far as God was concerned, the only viable route left was that of spiritual warfare. The men He had chosen to spearhead this warfare would be Moses and Aaron, using the rod. If the children of Israel were going to come out of Egypt free, then the Satanic princes that ruled over the land and held the people captive had to be dislodged from their place of control and influence in the heavenlies. Their thrones had to be destroyed.

• Over a period of nine months, God judged Egypt with ten plagues to break the spiritual, economic, and international power of the land. They came to pass in the following chronological order.

1. The waters of the mighty river Nile turned to blood.
2. Frogs covered the land.
3. People and animals were covered with lice.
4. The land was invaded by swarms of flies.
5. Egyptians livestock was devastated by disease.
6. Boils and sores broke out over the Egyptians and their animals
7. Crops and vegetation were destroyed by hail.

8. Locusts invaded the land.
9. Gross darkness covered Egypt for the space of three days.
10. The death angel killed the firstborn of Egypt, both man and beast.

The effect of these plagues on the land of Egypt was devastating. Even in these modern days of technological and scientific advancement, it is hard to see any of the world powers like the Unites States, Japan, or Britain surviving the sheer scale and size of this kind of judgment. For nine months Egypt clung on. Over the nine months, God was progressively weakening the holds of the principalities and powers that ruled over the land. Every time Aaron raised that rod to commence a plague, it signified the beginning of a bitter spiritual battle in the heavenlies. God was judging the entrenched powers there.

For the Egyptians buried all their first-born, which the LORD had smitten among them: upon their gods also the LORD executed judgments. **Numbers 33:4**

The physical effects of those judgments were manifested through the plagues, but the spiritual effects were even more devastating. Satan was losing his power and grip, not only over the land of Egypt, but also over the children of Israel held in bondage there.

Satan's Counterfeit

Even as Moses was the man effecting spiritual warfare in the heavenlies, Satan had his own men fighting to oppose the purposes of God with sorcery and the occult. Paul in his letter to Timothy states, *"Now Jannes and Jambres withstood Moses, so do these also resist the truth: men of corrupt minds, reprobate concerning the faith. But they shall proceed no further: for their folly shall be made manifest unto all men, as theirs also was."* *2 Timothy 3:8-9*

Moses and Aaron appeared before Pharaoh, and Aaron cast down his rod which turned into a snake.

Then Pharaoh also called the wise men and the sorcerers: now the magicians of Egypt, they also did in like manner with enchantments.

For they cast down every man his rod, they became serpents: but Aaron's rod swallowed up their rods. *Exodus 7:11-12*

Satan used the wise men and sorcerers, led by Jannes and Jambres, to mount up a resistance against God's purposes and plans by counterfeiting His works and trying to dilute the efficacy of God's power. When the waters of Egypt were turned into blood by Aaron's rod, Jannes and Jambres did the same with their enchantments. They proceeded to match the plague of frogs, as well.

When God starts to do something in a certain sphere, be it in the life of an individual, family, church, or nation, the enemy starts to fight it. The only way to get rid of the enemy is to continue to raise the stakes and mount more pressure on him in the realm of the spirit through accumulative prayer. This is exactly what Moses and Aaron did. Therefore, after the plague of frogs which the sorcerers of Egypt counterfeited, God gave more instructions to Moses.

And the LORD said unto Moses, Say unto Aaron, stretch out thy rod, and smite the dust of the land, that is may become lice throughout all the land of Egypt.

And they did so; for Aaron stretched out his hand with his rod, and smote the dust of the earth, and it became lice in man, and in beast; all the dust of the land became lice throughout all the land of Egypt.

And the magicians did so with their enchantments to bring forth lice, but they could not: there were lice upon man and upon beast.

Then the magicians said unto Pharaoh, This is the finger of God.   Exodus 8: 16-19

In every circumstance, Satan's abilities are finite. There is a limit to which he can extend himself and after that he just cannot operate. On the other hand, God's power and abilities are limitless. How interesting! After all the copycat methods of Jannes and Jambres using demonic power, they hit a blank wall and had to confess with their mouth, "This is the finger of God." Jesus, many years later when He was slandered that He had cast out devils through Beelzebub, the chief of the devils, made more powerful statements about the operation of the same finger of God about which Jannes and Jambres had referred:

But if I with the finger of god cast out devils, no doubt the kingdom of God is come upon you.

> *When a strong man armed keepeth his*
> *palace, his goods are in peace:*
> *But when a stronger than he shall come*
> *upon him. And overcome him, he taketh*
> *from him all his armour wherein he trusted,*
> *and divideth his spoils.   Luke 11:20-22*

We see Jesus state the fact that he cast out devils by the finger of Almighty God, and then He speaks further about spiritual warfare—that the enemy will not budge until someone stronger overcomes him and kicks him out. It is expedient that we wage war in the realm of the spirit to take back that which is ours and gain new territory in Jesus Christ.

•Even after the defeat of the sorcerers in Egypt, there was no let up in God's onslaught against the powers and principalities that ruled the land. Satan, under intense pressure, wanted a negotiated settlement. But God, through Moses and Aaron said, "No deal." The original demands stands fast; "Let my people go." And, the people had to come out of the land of Egypt with all their possessions and great wealth. Many times, we pray, putting the enemy under so great a pressure that he is forced to play one of his deceptive cards. He allows us to have a small breakthrough in the area we are praying about, just to get us to stop praying and relieve the pressure on him. It is a sad fact that many of us bite the bait, not realizing that we could have had a greater victory if we had tarried in the place of prayer.

Liberty Time

In Egypt, the plagues continued until the enemy was totally defeated and had to let the people go. Even then, Satan tried to counter attack at the shores of the Red Sea; and the same rod which had dealt so effectively against him was used to break that counter attack. At last, the prophecy which God had given to Abraham at the cutting of the covenant had come to pass — but through warfare. If Satan and his forces had not been challenged in the heavenlies, the people might never have come out of Egypt.

Exodus 12 makes some interesting reading after the epic events that had taken place.

Now the sojourning of the children of Israel, who dwelt in Egypt, was four hundred and thirty years.

And is came to pass at the end of the four hundred and thirty years, even the selfsame day it came to pass, that all the hosts of the LORD went from the land of Egypt.

Exodus 12:40-41

God had promised Abraham that the people would be in bondage four hundred years. But, the Scripture above makes it clear that they spent an extra thirty years in Egypt. This extra time in bondage should never have occurred. Satan tried desperately to hold the people in bondage, using every trick at his disposal, but failed in the end. For reasons that we will not discuss in this particular book, he had managed to delay God's purposes, but not abort them. In the end, spiritual warfare won the day; and the people came out of bondage. I strongly recommend that you prayerfully read the first fifteen chapters of the book of Exodus. A new word of spiritual warfare will be opened unto you.

Chapter Two

Possessing the Land

The issues that we have to deal with in this life are real. We have to appraise many, sometimes complex, issues and come to certain conclusions. Sometimes our conclusions can be flawed because being human, we are often limited and do not possess all the facts to be able to make proper judgments. This is the basic reason why we need God. Beyond this, we also need to live a life that is rooted in the Spirit of God.

> *This I say then, Walk in the Spirit, and ye*
> *shall not fulfill the lust of the flesh.*
> *Galatians 5:16*

The role of the Holy Spirit in keeping us within the purposes of God concerning our lives is vital. It is impossible to fight this warfare without Him. Since it is basically the Holy Spirit that declares God's purposes with regard to our lives, it is He that will help bring it to pass.

> *Likewise, the Spirit also helpeth our infirmities: for we know not what we should pray for as we ought: but the Spirit itself maketh intercession for us with groaning which cannot be uttered.*
>
> *And he that searcheth the hearts knoweth what is the mind of the Spirit, because he maketh intercession for the saints according to the will of God.* **Romans 8:26-27**

When the Holy Spirit enters the scene, the seemingly impossible in the natural now becomes possible. What we could not handle by our natural abilities become easy; because, the most powerful person in the universe has come on the scene. But, we must bear in mind that He comes to help us. There is a part that we have to play, and warfare prayer is a major element of it.

The children of Israel sadly missed this revelation after they left Egypt and entered the wilderness.

The repercussions of their failure cost them dearly. The unfortunate events we are about to examine and their aftermath need not have had to happen.

The Road to Disaster

And the LORD spake unto Moses, saying, Send thou men, that they may search the land of Canaan, which I give unto the children of Israel. **Numbers 13:1**

Moses, obeying the command of the LORD, dispatched twelve men, one chosen from each of the twelve tribes of Israel in the wilderness of Paran. For forty days, these men were away on a covert, intelligence gathering mission, investigating the land that God said He was to give them. It is interesting to follow the progress of these spies as they soak in vital social, military, and economic data pertaining to the land.

So they went up, and searched the land from the wilderness of Zin unto Rehob, as men come to Hamath.

And they ascended by the south, and came unto Hebron; where Ahiman, Sheshai, and Talmi, the children of Anak, were. (Now

Hebron was built seven years before Zoan in Egypt.)

And they came unto the brook of Eshcol, and cut down from thence a branch with one cluster of grapes, and they bare it between two upon a staff; and they brought of the pomegranates, and of the figs.

The place was called the brook of Eshcol, because of the cluster of grapes which the children of Israel cut down from thence.

Numbers 13:21-24

From the Biblical account to follow, it seems that the whole spy mission ended in disaster. There were the exceptions of Joshua and Caleb, however, who had an insight and foresight into the promises of God for the land.

And they went and came to Moses, and to Aaron, and to all the congregation of the children of Israel, unto the wilderness of Paran, to Kadesh; and brought back word unto them, and unto all the congregation, and showed them the fruit of the land.

And they told him, and said, We come unto the land whither thou sentest us, and surely it floweth with milk and honey; and this is the fruit of it.

Nevertheless the people be strong that dwell in the land, and the cities are walled, and very great: and moreover we saw the children of Anak there.

The Amalekites dwell in the land in the south: and the Hittites, and the Jebusites, and the Amorites, dwell in the mountains: and the Canaanites dwell by the sea, and the coast of Jordan.

And Caleb stilled the people before Moses, and said, Let us go up at once, and possess it; for we are well able to overcome it.

But the men that went up with him said, We be not able to go up against the people; for they are stronger than we.

And they brought up an evil report of the land which they had searched unto the children of Israel, saying, The land, through which we have gone to search it, is a land that eateth up the inhabitants thereof; and all the people that we saw in it are men of a great stature.

And there we saw the giants, the sons of Anak, which come of the giants: and we were in our own sight as grasshoppers and so we were in their sight.

Numbers 13:26-33

● In spite of Caleb's strong exhortations, the damage had been done. The people started murmuring against Moses and Aaron. Their actions provoked the LORD to such a degree, that it took strong intercession by Moses to turn away His wrath. In speaking to Moses afterwards, God revealed His mind concerning the situation.

Say unto them, As truly as I live, saith the LORD, as ye have spoken in mine ears, so will I do to you:

Your carcasses shall fall in this wilderness; and all that were numbered of you, according to your whole number, from twenty years and upward, which have murmured against me,

Doubtless ye shall not come into the land, concerning which I swore to make you dwell therein, save Caleb the son of Jephunneh, and Joshua the son of Nun.

But your little ones, which ye said should be a prey, them will I bring in, and they shall know the land which ye have despised.

But as for you, your carcasses, they shall fall in the wilderness.

And your children shall wander in the wilderness forty years, and bear your whore-doms, until your carcasses be wasted in the wilderness.

After the number of the days in which ye searched the land, even forty days, each day a year, shall ye bear your iniquities, even forty years and ye shall bear your iniqui-ties, even forty years, and ye shall know my breach of promise.   Numbers 14: 28-34

The next forty years were to witness the children of Israel wandering about in the wilderness. If they had fully taken hold of the promise of God and warred with it, they would have been dwelling in the land of promise.

We must realize that God means what He says and says what He means. He does not play around with His Word. If He has said it, then He will do it. We must bear in mind, also, that just because He has said it does not mean that we are free to sit down, fold our arms, and expect it to come to pass. We have to arm ourselves with these promises and wage a good warfare to see the manifestation of that which God has spoken. Caleb and Joshua caught the revelation that even though there were giants in the land of promise, God would still give them victory—only and when they would go into battle.

Many a time, we receive a promise from God and see great physical obstacles before us, which make the fulfillment of His Word in our lives look impossible. Despite those obstacles, God expects us to be strong in faith and wage a good warfare to bring about the manifestation of that which He has spoken.

Taking the Land

After years of wandering, God spoke to Moses:

Ye have compassed this mountain long enough: turn you northward.

Deuteronomy 2:3

He went on to tell them not to meddle with the Edomites because He had given Mount Seir (Edom) unto Esau for a possession. They were also not to distress the Moabites and Amonites because He had given Moab and Amon to the children of Lot for a possession. Then came a powerful promise:

Rise ye up, take your journey, and pass over the river Arnon: behold, I have given into thine hand Sihon the Amorite, king of Heshbon, and his land: begin to possess it, and contend with him in battle

Deuteronomy 2:24

For me, this Scripture is one of the most powerful in matters pertaining to birthing the promises of God in battle. Here, we see God telling the children of Israel that He had already given Sihon the Amorite, King of Heshbon, and his land to them. Then He gives them the key as to how to receive that which He has given. He tells them to begin to possess it and contend with Sihon the Amorite <u>in battle</u>. We can see now the relationship between possessing the land and warfare. God was effectively saying that His will for them was to have the land that belongs to Sihon, but they would have to engage him in battle to take that which was theirs. This time the children of Israel did not stagger at the promises of God. They <u>decided</u> to fight for that what was theirs.

- *Then Sihon came out against us, and he all his people to fight at Jahaz.*
Deuteronomy 2:32

43

Be warned, when you begin to pray into manifestation the promises and prophecies of God concerning you, the enemy will not just lie down and play dead. He will mount up a resistance. As exemplified by the above Scripture, Sihon and his armed forces came against the army of the children of Israel to fight.

> *And the LORD our God delivered him before us: and we smote him, and his sons and all his people.*
>
> *And we took all his cities at that time and utterly destroyed the men and the women and the little ones, of every city, we left nine to remain:*
>
> *Only the cattle we took for a prey unto ourselves and the spoil of the cities which we took.*
>
> *From Aroer, which is by the brink of the river of Arnon, and from the city that is by the river, even unto Gilead, there was not one city too strong for us: the LORD our God delivered all unto us.*
>
> *Deuteronomy 2:33-36*

We behold the end result. Just as the LORD God had promised, it came to pass—but with warfare!

◆ Now that the children of Israel had started to get the hang of how these principles operated, God gave them added opportunities to possess more land on the east bank of the Jordan river.

Then we turned, and went up the way to Bashan: and Og the king if Bashan came out against us, he and all his people, to battle at Edrei.

And the LORD said unto me, Fear not: for I will deliver him, and all his people, and his land, into thy hand; and thou shalt do unto him as thou didst unto Sihon, king of the Amorites, which dwelt at Heshbon.

So the Lord our God delivered into our hands Og also, the king of Bashan, and all his people: and we smote him until none was left to him remaining.

And we took all his cities at that time, there was not a city which we took not from them, threescore cities, all the region of Argob, the kingdom of Og in Bashan.

All these cities were fenced with high walls, gates, and bars; beside a great many towns without walls.

And we utterly destroyed them, as we did unto Sihon king of Heshbon, utterly destroying the men, women and children of every city.

But all the cattle, and the spoil of the cities, we took for a prey to ourselves.

And we took at that time out of the hand of the two kings of the Amorites the land that was on this side of Jordan, from the river of Arnon unto mount Hermon;

(Which Hermon the Sidonians call Sirion; and the Amorites call it Shenir;)

All the cities of the plain and all the Gilead, and all Bashan, unto Salchah and Edrei, cities of the kingdom of Og in Bashan.

For only Og king of Bashan remained of the remnant of giants; behold, his bedstead was a bedstead of iron; is it not in Rabbath of the children of Ammon? Nine cubits was the length thereof, and four cubits the breadth of it, after the cubit of a man.

Deuteronomy 3:1-11

The battle at Edrie which resulted in the defeat of Og the king of Bashan was no ordinary battle.

Og was a giant whose bedstead was thirteen and a half feet long and six feet wide. But disregarding his immense stature, the children of Israel warred against him and prevailed.

It is interesting to note that the fear of these same giants had kept the children of Israel nearly forty years prior to this battle from invading the land of Canaan. This time they ignored the enemy's strength and concentrated on the job at hand, believing and acting on the promise of God. As a direct result of those two battles with Sihon, king of Heshbon, and Og, king of Bashan, the children of Israel gained valuable land, which was given unto the tribes of Reuben, Gad, and half the tribe of Manasseh.

Be assured that if you wage effective warfare to bring to pass the purposes of God pertaining to your life, you will push back frontiers in the realm of the spirit and in the natural.

Chapter Three

A Man of Like Passions

M any of us find the call to pray through God's promises a daunting task. We get physically tired and discouraged if we seem to be making no headway. The sheer prospect of grueling hours of travail to give birth to the miracle makes the whole venture appear so difficult. However, as much as God understands our weaknesses, He still expects us to be to pray to gain the victory.

Elias was a man subject to like passions as we are, and he prayed earnestly that it might not rain: and it rained not on the earth by space of three years and six months.

And he prayed again, and the heaven gave rain and the earth brought forth her fruit.   *James 5:17*

In unambiguous terms, the Bible declares that the prophet Elijah had similar challenges to the ones that we go through. He faced fear, laziness, lethargy, bouts of prayerlessness, depression; and sometimes he grew discouraged. In spite of all these human frailties and setbacks, he had the trump card. He could pray.

And his mode of prayer was not something to satisfy a religious itch. The Bible makes us aware that he prayed earnestly. If there is a classical biblical case study of praying God's prophecies into manifestation, then Elijah's prayer life is the one most worthy of emulation.

And Elijah the Tishbite , who was of the inhabitants of Gilead, said unto Ahab, As the LORD God of Israel liveth, before whom I stand, there shall not be dew nor rain these years, but according to my word.

1 Kings 17:1

The Undercurrents

Israel was in trouble of a most serious kind. Idolatry was flourishing and seemed to be running unchecked. The Bible repeatedly declares the kings as on-going evil in the sight of the LORD. The then King Ahab, the son of Omri, was given this testimonial by God:

And Ahab the son of Omri did evil in the sight of the LORD above all that were before him.

And it came to pass, as if it had been a light thing for him to walk in the sins of Jeroboam the son of Nebat, that he took to wife Jezebel the daughter of Ethbaal king of the Zidonians, and went and served Baal, and worshiped him.

And he reared up an altar for Baal in the house of Baal, which he had built in Samaria.

And Ahab made a grove; and Ahab did more to provoke he LORD God of Israel to anger than all the kings of Israel that were before him.   *1 Kings 16:30-33*

Ahab's conduct was a recipe for national disaster. With Jezebel right by the seat of power, Baal had a strategically placed agent. So great was Jezebel's influence, that Ahab built an altar for Baal in the city of Samaria. Satan was working overtime to bring down God's people. In the midst of this apparent national backsliding, we see the appearance of a man about whom the Bible gives scanty details as to his origins or background.

The man's name was Elijah. He was a Tishbite who came from the region of Gilead on the east bank of the Jordan river. No indication is given of his age or his prophetic preparation; yet, he somehow managed to secure an audience with Ahab and declare a terse prophecy about a three-and-half-year famine. Much as he had prophetic insight into the purposes of God, he must have had the supportive base from God's word concerning the situation. In Deuteronomy 27:11-13, at mount Ebal, as part of the long declaration of that day, he pronounced the following curse over the children of Israel if they disobeyed the LORD:

And thy heaven that is over thy head shall be brass, and the earth that is under thee shall be iron.

> *The LORD shall make the rain of thy land*
> *powder and dust: from heaven shall it come*
> *down upon thee, until thou be destroyed.*
> *Deuteronomy 28:23-24*

One of the hallmarks of genuine divine prophecy is that it always has its root and basis from God's word. Be wary of prophecy that cannot be supported by the Bible. God would not say or do anything that falls outside the scope and boundaries of His word.

> *Beloved, believe not every spirit, but try*
> *the spirits whether they are of God: because*
> *many false prophets are gone out into the*
> *world.* *1 John 4:1*

Travail

It is important to note that the prophet Elijah did not just declare the prophecy to Ahab, walk out of the palace, and then go to sleep.

> *... and he prayed earnestly that it might*
> *not rain...* *James 5:17*

Elijah knew that, as God had said there was going to be the three and a half years of famine, the manifestation of the prophecy was going to come via prayer. The Bible declares that he prayed earnestly that it might not rain.

This kind of prayer is hard work. It calls for hours of travail. It means laying hold of God in prayer and not quitting until the result from Him is seen.

> *...ye that make mention of the LORD, keep not silence,*
> *And give him no rest, till he establish and till he make Jerusalem a praise in the earth.*　　　*Isaiah 6:6-7*

> *And there is none that calleth upon thy name that stirreth up himself to take hold of thee...*　　　*Isaiah 64: 7*

It is apparent that Elijah prayed the prophecy through. For we see it come to pass. The whole land was soon gripped by the drought and dryness which affected every segment of social and economic activity. Elijah, by the command of God, moved out of the borders of Israel to Zarephath, where he stayed with a poor widow. While there, God supernaturally sustained him and the window's family.

Meanwhile, as the famine bit even more viciously into Israel, the realization dawned on Ahab that the man who walked up to him in the palace in Samaria and declared that there was going to be a famine was no jester. The prophecy was for real. Elijah became the most sought after man in Israel. An international warrant was issued for his arrest. If it had been in today's world, he would have been on Interpol's computer network with his picture at every international airport and entry point.

And it came to pass after many days, that the word of the LORD came to Elijah in the third year, saying, Go show thyself unto Ahab; and I will send rain upon the earth.

1 Kings 18:1

Once again, we see God giving the exiled prophet a specific prophecy. Three years into the famine, God commands Elijah to make a bold appearance before the desperate Ahab; and He, God, will send rain upon the earth. Elijah makes the move and first meets Obadiah, Ahab's chief of staff, and then the king himself.

And it came to pass, when Ahab saw Elijah, that Ahab said unto him, Art thou he that troubleth Israel?

And he answered, I have not troubled Israel; but thou, and thy father's house in that ye have forsaken the commandments of the LORD, and thou hast followed Baalim.

Now therefore send, and gather to me all Israel unto mount Carmel, and the prophets of Baal four hundred and fifty, and the prophets of the groves four hundred, which eat at Jezebel's table.   *1 Kings 18: 17-19*

The scene was set for one for the most exciting power encounters in Israel's history. Not since the days of Moses, when he challenged the powers of Egypt, had anything so dramatic happened. In the ensuing episodes, Baal failed to manifest and deliver on that day. But, the LORD God did make spectacular display. In a dramatic show of power, He sent fire from heaven to consume the sacrifice, the wood, the stones, the dust, and the water in the trench. That day parts of the brook of Kishom turned red as the people, acting on Elijah's command, slaughtered the prophets of Baal at her banks. In the midst's of all this excitement on the summit of Carmel, after the showdown with Baal, there was one thing bubbling in Elijah's spirit and he soon let it out:

And Elijah said unto Ahab, Get thee up, eat and drink; for there is a sound of abundance of rain.   *1 Kings 18:41*

The prophet had given the king the go-ahead to declare, but the king was not about to do that. He had different business to attend to:

So Ahab went up to eat and drink, And Elijah went up to the top of Carmel; and he cast himself down upon the earth, put his face to his knees,
And said to his servant, Go up now, look toward the sea. And he went up, and looked, and said, There is nothing. And he said, Go again seven times.
And it came to pass on the seventh time, that he said, Behold, there ariseth a little cloud out of the sea, like a man's hand. And he said, Go up and say unto Ahab, Prepare thy chariot, and get thee down, that the rain stop thee not.
And it came to pass in the mean while, that the heaven was black with clouds and wind and there was a great rain. And Ahab rode, and went to Jezreel. 1 Kings 18: 43-45

In the first portions of this Scripture, we see the hallmarks of earnest prayer. The prophet cast himself upon the ground, tucked his head between his knees, and began to travail in prayer. All he was seeking was a manifestation of the prophecy that God was sending rain. A command to his servant to look towards the Mediterranean for any sign of rain yields a negative result, but the prophet did not quit. He persevered in travail to bring to birth that which God had promised.

The servant had to go seven times; and at the seventh observation, he saw the first physical manifestation of the spiritual travail of Elijah. He noticed a small could like that of a hand of a man rising out of the sea. Soon the sky darkened with great rain clouds accompanied by wind. The Biblical description of the subsequent downpour was "…a great rain."

We can glean much from Elijah's example. In the depth of travail, he refused to quit until he saw the physical manifestation of his earnest prayers. His servant had to do a seven-time check before he saw the faintest manifestation of a breakthrough. How often have we quit when God expected us to press on and achieve the breakthrough?

Chapter Four

Hezekiah's Great Deliverance

There are times in our Christian life when earnest, prevailing prayer is not even an option among a number of seemingly viable choices. Due to the sheer scale of the situation that confronts us, it is the **only** thing we can employ—if we are to survive. The fact of the matter is that prayer works **only** if we pray earnestly enough, according to God's counsel.

An Award-Winning King

We turn again to God's Word to see what a particular man did when Satan forced his back against the wall. He had virtually no options left—except one. The man was King Hezekiah. He faced a most life-threatening situation. In the long line of the twenty

Kings of Judah, from Rehoboam to Zedekiah, Hezekiah gets special mention in the Bible because of his response to his situation. Let us see:

He trusted in the LORD God of Israel; so that after him was none like him among all the kings of Judah, not any that were before him. *2 Kings 18:5*

For God to give him the award of being the best king Judah had ever produced must have meant that Hezekiah was special. Note that in God's eyes, he had to be better than Kings like Jehoshaphat and Josiah, who were no lightweights in their day.

Now it came to pass in the third year of Hoshea son of Elah king of Israel, that Hezekiah the son of Ahaz of Judah began to reign.

Twenty and five years old was he when he began to reign; and he reigned twenty and nine years in Jerusalem. His mother's name also was Abi, the daughter of Zachariah.

And he did that which was right in the sight of the LORD, according to all that David his father did.

He removed the high places, and brake the images, and cut down the groves, and brake in pieces the brazen serpent that Moses had made: for unto those days the children of Israel did burn incense to it: and he called it Nehushtan.   *2 Kings 18: 1-4*

The Bible describes him as having done that which was right in the sight of the LORD and dealing with idolatry in the land. One particular idol that he destroyed was the brazen serpent that Moses made in the wilderness. In the book of Numbers 21:6-9, God judged the people in the wilderness with fiery serpents which bit them; and many of the Israelites died as a result. After Moses' intercession before the LORD, God commanded him to make the brazen serpent and put it on a pole, so that whoever was bitten by one of the serpents could look upon the brazen serpent and live. Hundreds of years later, the people now regarded the serpent as an idol and worshipped it. Hezekiah, in this time, destroyed that brazen serpent.

When the Enemy Strikes

In the midst of all Hezekiah's service unto the LORD, Satan sent a most formidable challenge against him. The challenge was no ordinary one. Satan was determined to wipe out Judah from existence. The instrument he used to affect his purposes was the powerful Assyrian army commanded by King Sennacherib. This was no ordinary army. Under the command of King Sennacherib, the army had never lost a battle. Their reputation went before them.

Contemporary history records Assyrians as being an extremely cruel people. Some of their carvings and paintings in Nineveh, their capital, depicted captives hanged in batches, impaled on stakes, or flayed alive. They were a people who showed little or no mercy. Drawing on Satanic power from Nisroch, their god, they were about to use to destroy the people of the true God. When they launched their assault against the kingdom of Judah, targeting Jerusalem as the ultimate prize, King Hezekiah and all Judah knew that they had a serious situation confronting them.

Now in the fourteenth year of king Hezekiah, Sennacherib king of Assyria come up against all the fenced cities of Judah, and took them.

And Hezekiah kind of Judah sent to the king of Assyria to Lachish, saying, I have offended: return from me: that which thou puttest on me will I bear. And the king of Assyria appointed unto Hezekiah king of Judah three hundred talents of silver and thirty talents of gold.

And Hezekiah gave him all the silver that was found in the house of the LORD, and in treasures of the king's house.

At that time did Hezekiah cut off the gold from the doors of the temple of the LORD, and from the pillars which Hezekiah king of Judah had overlaid, and gave it to the king of Assyria.   *2 Kings 18:13-16*

We find that in the initial campaign, Sennacherib swept through Judah, capturing fenced city after fenced city. Hezekiah' response was appeasement. He decided to pay a heavy financial tribute to the Assyrian king. In today's money, the total tribute would be a little under one hundred and ninety million American dollars.

So strapped was the Judean treasury for cash that he did the most unthinkable. All the silver in the house of the LORD was given to the Assyrian king as well as the treasures in the king's house. That not being enough, the temple door and pillars were stripped of their inlaid gold decorations.

One thing we have to realize is that it is foolish to pay off the devil.

> *...but the tender mercies of the wicked are cruel.*   *Proverbs 12:10*

He will still torment you after you think you have obtained a semblance of peace. He has a violent savage character which cannot be tamed. Jesus described him as thief, killer, and destroyer. Those have been his characteristics right from the Garden of Eden, and he is not going to modify his agenda for your sake, even if you compromise.

It did not take too long for King Hezekiah to realize that all that tribute had been poured down the drain. Satan, working through Sennacherib, had a more insidious objective. He wanted Jerusalem and he wanted it badly. He was not going to be paid off with gold and silver. We pick up the story where Satan now threw out all diplomacy and made his bid:

> *And when Hezekiah saw that Sennacherib was come, and that he was purposed to fight against Jerusalem,*
> *He took counsel with his princes and his mighty men to stop the waters of the*

fountains which were without the city: and they did help him.

So there was gathered much people together, who stopped all the fountains, and the brook that ran through the midst of the land, saying, Why should the kings of Assyria come. And find much water?

Also he strengthened himself, and built up all the wall that was broken, and raised it up to the towers, and another wall without, and repaired Millo in the City of David, and made darts and shields in abundance.

And he set captains of war over the people and gathered them together to him in the street of the gate of the city, and spake comfortably to them, saying,

Be strong and courageous, be not afraid nor dismayed for the king of Assyria, nor for all the multitude that is with him: for there be more with us than with him:

With him is an arm of flesh; but with us is the LORD our God to help us, and to fight our battles. And the people rested themselves upon the words of Hezekiah king of Judah.

2 Chronicles 32: 2-8

• When it became clear that no tribute was going to stop Sennacherib, Hezekiah tried to do what he could in the natural. He had a war conference with his key advisors and generals on the best form of defense to take against an army that was yet to lose a battle. It was decided that the first strategy would be to deny the Assyrian army of drinking water, both army and beast.

Next, Jerusalem's perimeter defenses were repaired and strengthened. After that came a massive arms pile up. Finally, various captains and sector commanders were appointed for the city's defense. All these were natural measures taken against an enemy that was backed by satanic power.

Many a time, when we face a crisis, we do all that we can in the natural and still find that we are at our wits end, and that the situation had hardly changed. Then we start to apply spiritual measures. We see the same here with Hezekiah. After all the natural measures had been taken, he then moves seriously into the realm of the spirit. When he addresses the officers charged with coordinating the city defense, he charges them to be strong and courageous. He goes on to declare, as the prophet Elisha did years before, *"... for there be more with us than with him."* In this and subsequent statements, Hezekiah makes it abundantly clear that Judah's help will come from the LORD, who will fight her battles.

With that speech, a significant turning point occurred in the developing conflict. God had been brought into the picture and had taken Judah's side. The Bible declares that the people rested themselves upon the words of Hezekiah king of Judah. Encouraged by these words, Jerusalem's inhabitants waited for the dreaded threat of the Assyrian to materialize; and it did.

And the king of Assyria sent Tartan and Rabsaris and Rabshakeh from Lachish to king Hezekiah with a great host against Jerusalem. And they went up, they came down to Jerusalem. And when they were come up, they came and stood by the conduit of the upper pool, which is in the highway of the fuller's field.

And when they had called to the king, there come out to them Eliakim the son of Hilkiah, which was over the household, and Shebna the scribe, and Joah the son of Asaph the recorder. **2 Kings 18: 17-18**

While Sennacherib abided in Lachish, he sent a great army that encircled Jerusalem. To demonstrate the seriousness with which they attached to the conquest of that city, the invading army was commandeered by no less an officer that Tartan. In the Assyrian army, Tartan held the official title of the Commander-in-Chief, second only to the king. Accompanied with two ranking officials in Sennacherib's court, Tartan came close to the besieged city's outer defenses and was met by three of Hezekiah's high-ranking palace officials.

And Rabshakeh said unto them, Speak ye now to Hezekiah, Thus saith the great king, the king of Assyria, What confidence is this wherein thou trustest?

Thou sayest, (but they are but vain words), I have counsel and strength for the war. Now on whom dost thou trust, that thou rebellest against me?

Now, behold, thou trustest upon the staff of this bruised reed, even upon Egypt, on which if a man lean, it will go into his hand and pierce it: so is Pharaoh king of Egypt unto all that trust on him.

But if ye say unto me, We trust in the LORD our God: is not that he, whose high places and whose altars Hezekiah hath taken away, and hath said to Judah and

Jerusalem, Ye shall worship before this altar in Jerusalem?

Now therefore, I pray thee give pledges to my lord the king of Assyria, and I will deliver thee two thousand horses, if thou be able on thy part of set riders upon them.

How then wilt thou turn away the face of one captain of the least of my masters' servants, and put thy trust on Egypt for chariots and for horsemen?

Am I now come up without the LORD against this place to destroy it? The LORD said to me, Go up against this land, and destroy it.

Then said Eliakim the son of Hiljiah, and Shebna, and Joah, unto Rabshakeh, Speak, I pray thee, to thy servants in the Syrian language; for we understand it: and talk not with us in Jews' language in the ears of the people that are on the wall.

But Rabshakeh said unto them, Hath my master sent me to thy master, and to thee, to speak these words? Hath he not sent me to the men which sit on the wall that they may eat their own dung, and drink their own piss with you?

Then Rabshakeh stood and cried with a loud voice in the Jews' language, and spake, saying, Hear the word of the great king, the king of Assyria:

Thus saith the king, Let not Hezekiah deceive you: for he shall not be able to deliver you out of his hand:

Neither let Hezekiah make you trust in the LORD, saying, The LORD will surely deliver us, and this city shall not be delivered into the hand of the king of Assyria.

Hearken not to Hezekiah for thus saith the king of Assyria, Make an agreement with me by a present, and come out to me and then eat ye every man of his own vine, and every one of his fig tree, and drink ye every one the waters of his cistern:

Until I come and take you away to a land like your own land, a land of corn and wine, a land of bread and vineyards, a land of oil olive and of honey, that ye may live, and not die: and hearken not unto Hezekiah, when he persuadeth you saying, The LORD will deliver us.

Hath any of the gods of the nations delivered at all his land out of the hand of the king of Assyria?

Where are the gods of Hamath, and of Arpad? Where are the gods of Sepharvaim, Hena and Ivah? Have they delivered Samaria out of mine hand?

Who are they among all the gods of the countries, that have delivered their country out of mine hand, that the LORD should deliver Jerusalem out of mine hand?

But the people held their peace, and answered him not a word: for the king's commandment was, saying, Answer him not. 2 Kings 18:19-36

In the account we have just read, we find Sennecherib's envoys used a mixture of threats and deceptive offers to try and get the people of Jerusalem to rebel against Hezekiah's orders. We see Rabshakeh outline the alternatives that Hezekiah had at that moment. He either had to sign a defense pact with Egypt for Egyptian military force to help in the coming battle or trust in the LORD his God. He described the Egyptians as unreliable allies who would end up being a disappointment to Hezekiah. When it came to the things of God, though, Rabshakeh's knowledge appeared flawed. For having heard of Hezekiah tearing down the high places and altars in the land, he thought those high places were dedicated to Hezekiah's God. He inferred that God would not be able to deliver His people.

Next came a demand for more money if the invasion was to be stayed. So strong was Rabshakeh's confidence in the might of the Assyrian army that he said he would be able to provide two thousand spare horses if the kingdom of Judah could find riders for them. The boasts continued. Judah would not be able to prevail against even the least of Sennacherib's battle-hardened regiments.

So serious were Rabshakeh's threats and taunts that Hezekiah's envoys appealed to him to speak in Syrian, instead of the Jews' language, so that the faith of the men sitting on the wall would not be undermined. That appeal backfired as Rabshakeh shouted to those on the wall in the Jews' language, "Come away from trust in the LORD. He emphasized the fact that no nation's god protected that nation from the onslaught of this Assyrian army. He then reeled off a list of nations. So it was that even their God could not deliver His people. Little did Rabshakeh know that God had taken record of all his ridicule in Heaven.

Praying in a Crisis

When Hezekiah heard the report from his envoys, the spiritual tempo went up another notch.

> *And it came to pass, when king Hezekiah heard it, that he rent his clothes and covered himself with sackcloth, and went into the house of the LORD.*
>
> *And he sent Eliakim, which was over the household, and Shebna the scribe, and the elders of the priest, covered with sackcloth, to Isaiah the prophet the son of Amoz.*
>
> *And they said unto him, Thus saith Hezekiah, This day is a day of trouble, and of rebuke, and blasphemy: for the children are come to the birth, and there is not strength to bring forth.*   *2 Kings 19: 1-3*

After all is said and done, prayer is the most powerful weapon. Hezekiah was getting ready to call on the name of the LORD in earnest. Now was the time to call on the name of the LORD of hosts, the God of the armies of Israel. When the discouraging news was brought to him, he covered himself in sackcloth and went to the temple. He did not go into the temple to joke, he went in there to pray. However, he realized that the situation was so serious that prophetic utterances were needed to bring about a forceful turnaround. So he sent a message to Isaiah the prophet.

> *... for the children are come to the birth, and there is no strength to bring forth.*
> **2 Kings 19:3**

In effect he was telling the man of God that although we know that God will bring deliverance somehow, we also know that we have to travail in the spirit to bring it to pass. But we just do not have strength to travail.

> *Who hath heard such thing? Who hath seen such things? Shall the earth be made to bring forth in one day? or shall a nation be born at once? For as soon as Zion travailed, she brought forth her children. Isaiah 66:8*

In this Scripture, God makes clear that as soon as Zion, that is the Church or Christians, take time to travail earnestly in prayer, the breakthroughs they are believing in God will manifest. Now, Hezekiah was telling the prophet Isaiah that he was praying, but didn't have the strength to pray the kind of prayer that would cause the breakthrough to come about. Thank God for His word which declares:

> *Believe in the LORD your God, so shall ye be established, believe his prophets, so shall ye prosper.*   *2 Chronicles 20:20*

The prophet Isaiah sent a reply back to Hezekiah which was a prophecy from the LORD.

> *And Isaiah said unto them, Thus shall ye say to your master, Thus saith the LORD, Be not afraid of the words which thou hast heard, with which the servants of the king of Assyria have blasphemed me.*
>
> *Behold, I will send a blast upon him, and he shall hear a rumour, and shall return to his own land; and I will cause him to fall by the sword in his own land.*   *2 Kings 19: 6-7*

Rabshakeh, meanwhile, rejoined Sennacherib's forces as he fought against Libnah and proceeded to send serious threats by letter to Hezekiah.

> *And Hezekaih received the letter of the hand of the messengers, and read it: and*

Hezekiah went up into the house of the LORD, and spread it before the LORD.

And Hezekiah prayed before the LORD, and said, O LORD God of Israel, which dwellest between the cherubims, thou art the God, even thou alone, of all the kingdoms of the earth; thou hast heaven and earth.

2 Kings 19: 14-15

It is of supreme importance to note that Hezekiah, after receiving the letter, prayed before the LORD. That was where the breakthrough lay. He prayed so hard that Isaiah the prophet sent an even longer prophecy than the first concerning Judah and Jerusalem's deliverance to Hezekiah. The same night, because of prayer that had gone up to God from His people, an angel of the LORD was dispatched from heaven. When the angel had completed his mission, one hundred and eighty-five thousand Assyrian troops lay dead.

• In one night, the power of the so-called invincible Assyrian army was broken. That destruction came not by the weapons that Hezekiah had piled up in his earthly armory—but by prayer—which caused God to open His armory in heaven.

The LORD hath opened his armory and hath brought forth the weapons of his indignation. *Jeremiah 50:25*

So Sennacherib king of Assyria departed, and went and returned, and dwelt at Nineveh.
And it came to pass, as he was worshipping in the house of Nisroch his god, that Adrammelech and Sharezer his sons smote him with the sword: and they escaped into the land of Armenia. And Esarhaddon his son reigned in his stead. *2 Kings 19:36-37*

So ended the life of the king who Satan had tried to employ to destroy God's people. The failure came because of the power of prayer. And, thus the prophecy that Isaiah gave concerning Sennacherib's end came to pass.

Chapter Five

Prayer in the Palace

But thou, O Daniel, shut up the words,
and seal the book, even the time of the end:
many shall run to and fro, and knowledge
shall be increased.   *Daniel 12:4*

With that statement, an angel sent from God ends a long prophetic message that he had been giving to the prophet Daniel. After that, the angel would go on to answer two questions pertaining to the message he had just given. Of supreme importance was the fact that some of the deepest revelations from God of events yet to happen, spanning the period from the time of Alexander the Great to the Second Coming of Jesus and its aftermath, had been delivered to a man.

How did Daniel end up receiving this loaded prophecy in the first place? What was the sequence of events that led to his receiving these awesome words from God? To answer these questions, let us dig into the history of the man Daniel, his life and lifestyle.

Destined for Greatness

Daniel and Joseph, the son of Jacob, were two popular characters in the Bible about whom nothing negative was written. Both of them held high political office in foreign lands and died there. Whereas, Joseph married and bore two sons, Ephraim and Manasseh; there is no biblical record of Daniel having ever been married.

In 605 B.C., Babylonian military forces defeated the Egyptian army at Carchemish.

Against Egypt, against the army of Pharaohchnecho king of Egypt, which was by the river Euphrates in Carchemish, which Nebuchadnezzar king if Babylon smote in the fourth year of Jehoiakim the son of Josiah king of Judah.

Jeremiah 46: 2

With this conquest of Egypt, Babylon became the ruling superpower in the entire Middle East, having subdued Assyria a few years earlier. In that same year, Nebuchadnezzar brought the Kingdom of Judah, with its king, Jehoiakim, under his subjection. Jerusalem, the capital, was destroyed in three stages. In the first stage, Nebuchadnezzar carried off some members of the royal family, including Daniel, Shadrach, Meshach, and Abednego, into captivity in Babylon. In the second stage, about eight years later, he carried off Jehoiachin, the son of Jehoiakim, into Babylon with ten thousand captives.

Jehoiachin was eighteen years old when he began to reign and he reigned in Jerusalem three months. And his mother's name was Nehushta, the daughter of Elnathan of Jerusalem.

And he did that which was evil in the sight of the LORD according to all that his father had done.

At that time the servants of Nebuchadnezzar king of Babylon came up against Jerusalem, and the city was besieged.

And Nebuchadnezzar king of Babylon came against the city, and his servants did besiege it.

And Jehoiachin the king of Judah went out to the king of Babylon, he and his mother, and his servants, and his princes, and his officers: and the king of Babylon took him in the eighth year of his reign.

And he carried out thence all the treasures of the household the LORD, and the treasures of the kings' house, and cut in pieces all the vessels of gold which Solomon king of Israel had made in the temple of the LORD, as the LORD had said.

And he carried away all Jerusalem, and all the princes, and all the mighty men of valour, even ten thousand captives, and the craftsmen and smiths: none remained, save the poorest sort of the people of the land.

And he carried away Jehoiachin to Babylon, and the king's mother, and the king's wives, and his officers, and the mighty of the land, those carried into captivity from Jerusalem to Babylon.

And all the men of might, even seven thousand, and craftsmen and smiths a thousand, all that were strong and apt for war,

even them the king of Babylon brought
captive to Babylon.   *2 Kings 24:8-16*

After the forced emigration of the second stage, Nebuchadnezzar made Zedekiah, Jehoiachin's brother, king over Judah. Eleven years into Zedekiah's reign, Nebuchadnezzar, after a long siege because of Zedekiah's rebellion, destroyed Jerusalem bringing to completion the third and final stage.

Zedekiah was twenty and one years old when the began to reign, and he reigned eleven years in Jerusalem. And his mother's name was Hamutal, the daughter of Jeremiah of Libnah.

And he did that which was evil in the sight of the LORD, according to all the Jehoiakim had done.

For through the anger of the LORD it came to pass in Jerusalem and Judah, until he had cast them out from his presence, that Zedekiah rebelled against the king of Babylon.

And it came to pass in the ninth year of his reign, in the tenth month, in the tenth day of the month, that Nebuchadnezzar king of

Babylon came, he and all his host, against Jerusalem, and pitched against it: and they built forts against it round about.

And the city was besieged unto the eleventh year of king Zedekiah.

And on the ninth day of the fourth month the famine prevailed in the city, and there was no bread for the people of the land.

And the city was broken up, and all the men of war fled by night by the way of the gate between two walls, which is by the king's garden, (now the Chaldees were against the city round about:) and the king went the way toward the plain.

And the army of the Chaldees pursued after the king, and overtook him in the plains of Jericho: and all his army were scattered from him.

So they took the king, and brought him up to the king of Babylon to Riblah; and they gave judgment upon him.

And they slew the sons of Zedekiah before his eyes, and put out the eyes of Zedekiah, and bound him with fetters of brass and carried him to Babylon.

2 Kings 24:18 – 2 Kings 25:7

By the time of the third wave of destruction of Jerusalem by Nebuchadnezzar, Daniel had been away from the city for about nineteen years and was already exercising great political and administrative authority in Babylon. He had fared well in Babylon after he had left Jerusalem with the first wave of royal captives. Nebuchadnezzar enrolled Daniel, Shadrach, Meshach, and Abednego in a school for promising youths, that after their three-year course, they would be employed in the king's service. Daniel was given the name Belteshazzar, by the prince of eunuchs who looked after them. Originally, Shadrach, Meshach and Abednego had Hebrew names, Hananiah, Mishael, and Azariah; but these were changed to the Babylonian ones.

As for these four children, God gave them knowledge and skill in all learning and wisdom: and Daniel had understanding in all visions and dreams.

Now at the end of the days that the king had said he should bring them in, then the prince of the eunuchs brought them in before Nebuchadnezzar.

And the king communed with them; and among them all was found none like Daniel,

Hananiah, Mishael, and Azariah: therefore stood they before the king.

And in all the matters of wisdom and understanding, that the king inquired of them, he found them ten times better than all the magicians and astrologers that were in all his realm.   *Daniel 1:17-20*

About two years after Daniel first entered Babylon, he interpreted a difficult dream for Nebuchadnezzar after he and his three friends had sought the face of God.

Then the king made Daniel a great man, and gave him many great gifts, and made him ruler over the whole province of Babylon, and chief of the governors over all the wise men of Babylon.

Then Daniel requested of the king, and he set Shadrach, Meshach, and Abednego, over the affairs of the province of Babylon: but Daniel sat in the gate of the king.

    Daniel 2:48-49

By the time the second wave of forced émigrés came from Judah, six years after Daniel's appointment, he was a "well connected" official high up in the Babylonian establishment. In the line of duty, Daniel was to see his three friends miraculously survive being known into a fiery furnace and king Nebuchadnezzar making his dwelling with the beasts of the field for seven years. One of the final things that Daniel was to do under the Babylonian empire, was to interpret the writing on the wall, MENE, MENE, TEKEL, and UPHARSIN, which appeared to Belshazzar, the son of Nebuchadnezzar.

In that night was Belshazzar the king of Chaldeans slain.
And Darius the Median took the kingdom, being about threescore and two years old.
Daniel 5:30-31

Although the Medo-Persian were now in control, having destroyed the Babylonian empire, Daniel rose in political power.
It pleased Darius to set over the kingdom an hundred and twenty princes, which should be over the whole kingdom;
And over these presidents; of whom Daniel was first, that the princes might give account unto them, and the king should have no damage.

Then this Daniel was preferred above the presidents and princes, because an excellent spirit was in him; and the king thought to set him over the whole realm.   Daniel 6:1-3

A Man of Prayer

From the little detail gleaned about Daniel's life, we see his rise and conduct in the political establishment of first, the Babylonians, and then the Persians. Politics, however, was a small part of what the man was really about. From God's standpoint, he had a most important calling — that of prayer and intercession.

Daniel was real "heavy" when it came to prayer. In spite of his grueling secular schedule, there were few people in the Bible who could match his commitment to prayer and intercession. Through prayer, he was able to buy into the mind of God on matters pertaining to his generation and subsequent ones. After he became first president of the Medo-Persian empire, it was the daily habit of praying three times a day, facing Jerusalem, that led his being thrown into a den of lions. God delivered him from that satanically-inspired trap.

So this Daniel prospered in the reign of Darius, and in the reign of Cyrus the Persian.　　　　*Daniel 6:28*

To examine in detail this great man's prayer life would be a monumental task. Instead, we shall look at one situation pertaining to his ability in birthing the promises of God in battle. God spoke some powerful words to the prophet Jeremiah, which read:

Call unto me, and I will answer thee, and shew thee great and mighty things, which thou knowest not.　　　　*Jeremiah 33:3*

Although these words were spoken to Jeremiah, Daniel was accustomed to operating in the realm of calling upon the LORD for revelation concerning mighty things that the LORD was yet to do. Three years into the reign of Cyrus, king of the vast Persian empire, Daniel embarked on the most interesting fast.

In the third year of Cyrus king of Persia a thing was revealed unto Daniel, whose name was called Belteshazzar; and the thing was true, but the time appointed was long: and he understood the thing, and had understanding of the vision.

In those days I Daniel was mourning three full weeks.

I ate no pleasant bread, neither came flesh nor wine in my mouth, neither did I anoint myself at all, till three whole weeks were fulfilled.

And in the four and twentieth day of the first month, as I was by the side of the great river, which is Hiddekel;

Then I lifted up mine eyes, and looked, and behold a certain man clothed in linen, whose loins were girded with fine gold of Uphaz:

His body also like the beryl, and his face as the appearance of lightning, and his eyes as lamps of fire, and his arms and his feet like in color to polished brass, and the voice of a multitude.

And I Daniel alone saw the vision: for men that were with me saw not the vision; but a great awakening fell down them, so that they fled to hide themselves.

Therefore I was left alone, and saw this great vision, and there remained not strength *in me: for my comeliness was turned in me into corruption, and I retained no strength.*

Yet heard I the voice of his words: and when I heard the voice of his word, then was I in a deep sleep on my face, and my face toward the ground.

And, behold, an hand touched, which set me upon knees and upon the palms of my hands.

And he said unto me, O Daniel, a man greatly beloved, understand the words that I speak unto thee, and stand upright: for unto thee am I now sent. And when he had spoken this word unto me, I stood trembling.

Then said he unto me, Fear not, Daniel: for from the first day that thou didst set thine heart to understand, and to chasten thyself before thy God, thy words were heard, and I am come for thy words.

But the prince of the kingdom of Persia withstood me one and twenty days: but, lo, Michael, one of the chief princes, came to help me; and I remained there with the kings of Persia.

Now I am to make thee understand what shall befall thy people in the latter days: for the vision is for many days. Daniel 10:1-14

In the account just given, we see Daniel going on a twenty-one day fast, seeking some words from God pertaining to the things that would befall his people in the future. At the end of the third week, he is by the great river Hiddekel, otherwise known as the Tigris in modern days and now flowing in the nation of Iraq. By the banks of the river, he beholds a most terrible sight—that of an angel coming right out of spiritual warfare with the ruling Satanic prince over the Persian empire. So savage had been the fight in the heavenlies over Persian that the angel is described as having a face that looked like lightening, eyes that blazed like lamps of fire, arms and feet like that of colored brass. That should give you an idea of how fierce we have to be in the spiritual realm when we engage in combat. So terrible was the angle to behold that Daniel fainted. After he had been resuscitated, the angel made a crucial statement.

But the prince of the kingdom of Persia withstood me one and twenty days: but, lo, Michael, one of the chief princes came to help me; and I remained there with the kings of Persia.   *Daniel 10:13*

On the way from heaven with the message for Daniel, the prince of Persia, the satanic principality that controlled the entire Persian empire, intercepted the angel, trying to deter him. Daniel was on earth praying, adhering to the principle to pray ceaselessly until the answer comes.

For we wrestle not against flesh and blood, but against principalities, against powers, against the rulers of the darkness of this world, against spiritual wickedness in high places,   *Ephesians 6:12*

Unknown to him, it was his prayer that was keeping the angel strong in the face of great satanic opposition in the heavenlies. So strong was his prayer unto God that the archangel Michael was sent to reinforce the angel. Together, they managed finally to break through the satanic blockade. The whole battle in the spiritual realm had lasted for a full twenty-one days. During all that time, the man Daniel was in intense prayer fasting.

If Daniel had quit before that time, the angel sent from God might not have been able to break through the satanic resistance and would have returned back to heaven without completing his mission!

In Luke 18:1, Jesus said that, *"Men ought always to pray and not to faint."* So many times we start to pray for a breakthrough in a particular area and quit after a few days. The principle, however, is to continue praying until we see the manifestation of that which we are praying for. There is no simple way out. We have to tarry in the place of prayer until the back of the enemy is broken. Then the answer comes. God expects us to fight and bring His promises into fruition. That can only be achieved through intense prayer.

After the angel had told Daniel about the battle he had just come from he announced:

> *Now I am come to make thee understand what shall befall thy people in the latter days: for yet the vision is for many days.*
> *Daniel 10:14*

Before the angel proceeded to give the long prophecy we referred to at the beginning of this chapter, he made a strange statement:

> *Then said he, Knowest thou wherefore I come unto thee? And now will I return to fight with the prince of Persia: and when I*

am gone forth, lo, the prince of Gracia shall come.

The angel was telling Daniel that after giving the message, he would have to go back to fight the prince of Persia one more time. Put simply, he was depending on Daniel's prayer input to help defeat that satanic prince. He added that after the prince of Persia was dealt with, a new principality, the prince of Grecia, would rear up its head over that region. It is interesting to note that after the Persian empire, came the Greek empire. In the last of three great battles, Greek military forces, commanded by Alexander the Great, crossed the Euphrates river and defeated the Persian army Arbela in 331 B.C.

The angel then went on to give the extended prophecy from the LORD. We can read the account in the eleventh and twelfth chapters of the book of Daniel. The deep revelation did not come about by Daniel sleeping. It came through twenty-one days of intensive, sustained prayer with fasting. Remember! Nothing happens until we pray!

Chapter Six

Praying in the Messiah

In Chapter One, we had a small glimpse of Satan's attempt to cut off the infant Jesus from the face of the earth. That attempt came, after Joseph was warned in a dream by an angel to flee into the land of Egypt with Mary and Jesus. Escape was provided from the demonically-inspired command ordering that all children below the age of two in Bethlehem and its environs should be annihilated. In the terrible slaughter that followed the flight of Jesus into Egypt, many children were killed. Over five hundred years before this massacre took place, Jeremiah the prophet prophesied about this event saying:

Thus saith the LORD; A voice was heard in Ramah, lamentation, and bitter weeping; Rachel weeping for her children refused to be comforted for her children, because they were not. ***Jeremiah 31:15***

It was not by accident that the infant Jesus escaped this slaughter that was targeted at Him. There was a fundamental reason why He escaped. Prayer went forth on His behalf in advance. Yes! As you will discover later in this chapter, even Jesus, the son of God needed prayer cover to operate. If that all important prayer cover was absent when the forces of darkness struck through Herod, the consequences and effects of their success are unthinkable.

It is obvious that prayer is answered by the Father who sits on His mighty throne in heaven. However, He has decided to move and show forth His great and awesome power only when His people lift up their hands and pray unto Him. Even when it comes to matters concerning His Only Begotten Son, the rules were not changed. Prayer had to be offered up unto Him by His people in order for Him to respond.

There were, and still remain, a number of options open to the Father which will guarantee that His people will lift up holy hands unto Him in prayer.

He can, for example, put a burden of prayer on them concerning a certain situation through the action of the Holy Ghost. He can create circumstances in their lives which will ultimately lead them to fall on their knees and offer up prayer unto Him. The fact still remains that He needs a man or woman to pray unto Him to facilitate His mighty response.

From the eternal past, it was certain that Jesus would have to come unto Earth to die on the behalf of fallen man in order to reconcile him back with God.

> *... the Lamb slain from the foundation of the world.*   *Revelation 13:8*

So even before the creation of man, God, knowing the future, had already made a provision for man's fall.

Rebellion in Heaven

Before man was created, a crisis of a very serious kind took place in heaven that sowed the seeds of man's eventual fall. Lucifer, the archangel responsible for praise and worship in heaven, rebelled against God and tried to be like the Most High. The

Holy Ghost through the prophet Isaiah gives us an idea of what happened.

> *How art thou fallen from heaven, O Lucifer, son of the morning! How art thou cut down to the ground, which didst weaken the nations!*
>
> *For thou hast said in thine heart, I will ascend into the heaven, I will exalt my throne above the stars of God: I will sit also upon the mount of the congregation, in the sides of the north:*
>
> *I will ascend above the heights of the clouds; I will be like the Most High.*
>
> *Yet thou shalt be brought down to hell, to sides of the pit.*   *Isaiah 14:12-15*

The Holy Ghost gives us more insight into events that took place in the failed coup d'etat led by Satan.

> *Thou hast been in Eden the garden of God: every precious stone thy covering, the sardius, topaz, and the diamond, the beryl, the onyx, and the jasper, the sapphire, the emerald, and carbuncle, and gold: the workmanship of thy tabrets and of thy pipes was*

prepared in thee in the day that thou wast created.

Thou art the anointed cherub that covereth; and I have set thee so: thou wast upon the holy mountain of God; thou hast walked up and down the midst of the stones of fire.

Thou wast perfect in thy ways from the day that thou wast created till iniquity was found in thee.   *Ezekiel 28:13-15*

So serious was Satan's rebellion against God that he managed to enlist the support of one third of the angelic host in heaven.

And there appeared another wonder in heaven; and behold a great red dragon, having seven heads and ten horns, and seven crowns upon his heads.

And his tail drew the third part of the stars of heaven.   *Revelation 12:7-8*

In the ensuing eviction battle, God left the job of throwing Satan and his angels out of heaven to Michael, the archangel.

And there was war in heaven: Michael and his angels fought against the dragon; and the dragon fought and his angels,

And prevailed not; neither was their place found any more in heaven.

Revelation 12:7-8

By the time of man's creation, Satan, entrenched in his thinking to oppose the purposes of God at every opportunity, was ready to destroy God's ultimate creation—man. In the Garden of Eden he caused Adam to disobey God's commandment, and thus man fell. As a result of man's fall, the dominion that God had given him fell into Satan's hands.

Later, when Satan tried to get the LORD Jesus to compromise and worship him after Jesus' forty day fast in the wilderness, he made the following statement:

And the devil, taking him up into an high mountain, showed unto him all the kingdoms of the world in a moment of time.

And the devil said unto him, All this power will I give thee, and the glory of them: for that is delivered unto me; and to whomsoever I will I give it.

If thou wilt worship me, all shall be thine.   *Luke 4: 5-7*

In effect, Satan was telling Jesus that the power and the dominion that Adam lost was now his, that he could do anything he wanted to do with it. But right from the Garden of Eden, Satan had nursed a major problem. In the Garden, God Himself had spoken a powerful prophecy against him.

And I will put enmity between thee and the woman and between thy seed and her seed; it shall bruise thy head, and thou shalt bruise his heel.   *Genesis 3:15*

Satan was not going to stand by idly and wait for the seed of the woman to come and bruise his head. But the problems that confronted him were of a most complex kind. From where was the seed of the woman going to appear? How could He be located?

As an ex-archangel, he is restricted in his abilities. Unlike God, he is not omnipotent—that is, he does not have all the power. God has all power to do whatever He desires. Satan, on the other hand, being a created being, cannot do so. Boundaries and restrictions are set upon him, which he is powerless to circumvent.

Secondly, he is not omniscient—that is, he is not all knowing. God, who is omniscient, knows everything in the universe. Satan does not have that ability. Compared to God, he is severely limited in his knowledge.

Finally, God is omnipotent—that is, He can be everywhere at once. Satan cannot. He has to move from place to place.

Being now the god of this world, but aware of his limitations, Satan decided to infiltrate every family on the face of the earth with familiar spirits and build a complex intelligence and information-gathering network that would report to him. Principalities and powers were set over nations, cities, towns, and geographic locations. They in turn control hordes of demon spirits assigned to harass, oppress, and bind people. At every sphere in human existence, the enemy sought to infiltrate and control.

By his calculation, Satan has one big plus. Due to Adam's sin, every human being born is already tainted with sin. Paul, writing to Christians taken out of Satan's control through their rebirth in Christ, had this to say:

And you hath he quickened, who were dead in trespasses and sins:

Wherein in time past ye walked according to the course of this world, according to the prince of the power of the air, the spirit that now worketh in the children of disobedience:

Among whom also we all had our conversation in the times past in the lusts of our flesh, fulfilling the desires of the flesh and of the mind; and were by nature the children of wrath even as others.   Ephesians 2:1-3

As God sits in heaven, He is not worried for one moment about the empire-building dream of Satan. At the end of the day, they (God and Satan) are not in the same class.

Satan can make all his boasts and carry pompous pretensions, but he will never match God in any sphere. The best He can do is a weak copying of God.

Messianic Prophecies

Ever since the fall of man, God has been looking forward to the time of man's redemption from the power of sin and the devil. However, He is not about to be rushed. Redemption for man will have to come at an appointed time. Over a long time span, the Holy Ghost used men to declare different aspects of the coming of Jesus to Earth and the redemptive work that He would accomplish.

> *For the prophecy come not in time by the will of man: but holy men of God spake as they were moved by the Holy Ghost,*
> *2 Peter 1:21*

Some of the things that these prophets spoke of were quite straightforward; but others were difficult to understand, even to the prophets who prophesied them.

> *Of which salvation the prophets have inquired and searched diligently, who prophesied of the grace that should come unto you.* *1 Peter 1:10*

Whether the prophesies were understood or not, they kept coming in. Some of the vessels were Moses, Balaam, Isaac, David, Jeremiah, Isaiah, Daniel, Hosea, Micah, Zechariah and Malachi. If you diligently study the scores of prophecies about Jesus in the Old Testament, you can literally write about the high points of His entire life without refer-ring to the Gospels. Such was the depth of informa-tion God gave years before the Messiah came. In spite of the proliferation of prophecy, Satan was still groping in the dark. Some of the prophecies were simply too deep for him to fathom.

But we speak the wisdom of God in mystery, even the hidden wisdom, which God ordained before the world unto your glory:
1 Corinthians 2:7

...which things the angels desire to look into. *1 Peter 1:12*

At this point, it would be worthwhile for us to look at a few of the prophecies that were foretold concerning Jesus in the Old Testament.

Balaam

I shall see him, not now: I shall behold him, but not nigh: there shall come a star out of Jacob, and a Scepter shall rise out of Israel, and shall smite the corners of Moab, and destroy all the children of Sheth.
Numbers 24:17

PRAYING THROUGH THE PROMISES OF GOD

Isaac

The scepter shall not depart from Judah, nor a lawgiver from between his feet, until Shiloh come; and unto him shall the gathering of the people be.   *Genesis 49:10*

Moses

The LORD thy God will raise unto thee a Prophet from the midst of thee, of thy brethren, like unto me, unto him ye shall hearken.   *Deuteronomy 18: 15*

Isaiah

Therefore the LORD himself shall give you a sign; Behold, a virgin shall conceive, and bear a son, and shall call his name Immanuel.   *Isaiah 7:14*

For unto us a child is born, a son is given: and the government and peace there shall be no end, upon the throne of David, and upon his kingdom. To order it, and to establish it with judgment and with justice from

henceforth even forever. The zeal of LORD
of hosts will perform this.   Isaiah 9:6-7

The Intercessors

*As we have learned earlier, the fact that God gives prophecy does not mean it will automatically come to pass. It has to be prayed into fulfillment. Even the prophecies concerning Jesus in the Old Testament had to be prayed through into manifestation. In the New Testament, we discover two people who were crucial in giving Jesus the necessary prayer cover He needed, especially as an infant, to survive the moves of the enemy to eliminate Him from planet Earth.

And when the days of purification according to the law of Moses were accomplished, they brought him to Jerusalem, to present him to the Lord;

(As it is written in the law of the Lord, Every male that openeth the womb shall be called holy to the Lord;)

And to offer a sacrifice according to that which is said in the law of the Lord, a pair of turtledoves, or two young pigeons.

And, behold there was a man in Jerusalem, whose name was Simeon; and the same man was just and devout, waiting for the consolation of Israel: and the Holy Ghost was upon him.

And it was revealed unto him by the Holy Ghost, that he should not see death, before he had seen the Lord's Christ.

And he came by the Spirit into the temple: and when the parents brought in the child Jesus, to do for him after the custom of the law,

Then took he him in his arms and blessed God, and said, according to thy word:

For mine eyes have seen thy salvation,

Which thou hast prepared before the face of all people;

A light to lighten the gentiles and the glory of thy people Israel.

And Joseph and his mother marveled at those things which were spoken of him.

And Simeon blessed them, and said unto Mary his mother, Behold, this child is set for the fall and rising again of many in Israel; and for a sign which shall be spoken against;

(Yea, a sword shall pierce through thy own soul also,) that the thoughts of many hearts may be revealed.

And there was one Anna, a prophetess, the daughter of Phanuel, of the tribe of Aser: she was of a great age, and had lived with a husband seven years from her virginity;

And she was widow of about fourscore and four years which departed not from the temple, but served God with fasting and prayers night and day.

And she coming in that instant gave thanks likewise unto the Lord, and spoke of him to all that looked for redemption in Jerusalem. Luke 2:21-40

The above account is simply fascinating. We find that the baby Jesus, in order for all righteousness to be fulfilled, had to be presented to the LORD in the temple. And there this series of amazing events took place in the rapid succession.

A man named Simeon, who the Bible describes as "just and devout," walked into the temple at the same time as the young Jesus was being presented unto the LORD. The Bible further goes on to say that Simeon was waiting for the consolation of Israel and that the Holy Ghost was upon him.

It is important to realize that in the days of Simeon, the word of the LORD was very scarce in Israel. In fact, there had been a silence over four hundred years from the days of the prophet Malachi to the period six months before Jesus was born, when the angel Gabriel had appeared before Zachariah the father of John the Baptist in the temple. In that long period of time, the Bible is silent about God speaking to His people. Yet in the midst of the lack of the sure word of the LORD, we find a man upon whom the Holy Ghost rested. Even more crucially, because of the particular diligence he attached to "watching" for the Messiah's appearance, God had given him a personal word. He would not die until he saw the LORD's Christ!

Simeon was one of the secret weapons God had in Israel praying in the Messiah. He, having read of the prophecies, was not going to just fold his arms and wait for the promised Messiah. He willingly prayed to God about the Messiah's coming, constantly referring God to the many and powerful things that He had said about him. In the end, Simeon and others had accumulated enough prayer in heaven to cause God to release The Word to earth at the appointed time.

In the beginning was the Word, and the Word was with God, and the Word was God. **John 1:1**

And the Word was made flesh, and dwelt among us, (and we beheld his glory, the glory as of the only begotten of the Father,) full of grace and truth. **John 1:14**

But when the fullness of time was come, God sent forth his Son, made of a woman, made under the law... **Galatians 4:4**

By the time Jesus was presented in the temple, the Holy Ghost had been already at work coordinating important, divinely-ordained appointments.

And he came by the Spirit into the temple... **Luke 2:27**

Simeon was a very spiritual man. No poster had been put up in Jerusalem that Jesus would be coming into the temple that day. But as the child was brought in, lo and behold, Simeon appeared on the scene. Only the prompting of the Spirit could have brought him there at that hour. Entering, he took the young child in his arms, blessed God for the mighty breakthrough, and declared the following:

> *... **LORD**, now lettest thou thy servant depart in peace, according to thy word; For mine eyes have seen thy salvation.*
>
> *Luke 2:29-30*

In effect Simeon was saying, "My job is over. Now I can depart." Even as he was blessing the parents and the young child and giving Mary a prophecy, something dramatic happened, Anna the prophetess walked in. After a seven-year marriage, she has been a widow for a staggering eighty-four years. She is described as not departing from the temple, but serving God with fasting and prayers night and day. Here was a mighty woman of prayer. And like Simeon, she was so spiritual that she walked in at the right time to see the fruit of her travail. The sheer awe and awareness of who this little baby was must have electrified them!

Other visitors to the temple that day might have looked at Jesus and thought, "Oh, what a nice baby! Look at his hair. Oh, he is so good, he hardly ever cries." But Simeon and Anna knew what most people then could not know. The Savior of the world was well and truly on planet Earth. They knew that in some years to come He would shake Jerusalem to its foundations.

Israel would witness signs, wonders, and miracles — unprecedented in her history. Moses, Elijah, Elisha, and prophets, major and minor, had done their part But, this was going to be different. This time the Son of God would be at work. The level of anointing present that day in the temple must have been awesome. For those two intercessors, the reality of history being accomplished before their own eyes must have awakened great joy in them. As the Bible says about Jesus:

> *He shall see the travail of his soul, and shall be satisfied.*　　　　*Isaiah 53:11*

Before Simeon and Anna was the result of long periods of prayer and fasting, and it brought a euphoric feeling of great contentment. Remember, nothing happens until we pray! *Amen.*

Chapter Seven

Looking Unto Jesus

In the preceding chapters, we have see examples of how various individuals prayed through the purposes of God concerning diverse situations. We saw among others the tenacity of Elijah, the deep consistency of Daniel, and the epic prayer lives of Simeon and Anna. All these serve as examples to us. However, it is important to realize that all their heroic exploits pale in comparison to the achievements of an individual about whom John the Baptist had this to say:

He it is, who coming after me is preferred before me, whose shoe's latchet I am not worthy to unloose.   *John 1:27*

That person was none other than the LORD Jesus Christ. His prayer life was without equal in the entire Bible. For us Christians, the ultimate example that we need to emulate in the realm of the prophetic is the LORD Jesus Himself.

> *Wherefore seeing we also are compassed about with so great a cloud of witnesses, let us lay aside every weight, and the sin which doth so easily beset us, and let us run with patience the race that is set before us,*
> *Looking unto Jesus the author and the finisher if our faith.*   *Hebrews 12:1-2*

Even in the realm of prayer, Jesus has to be our focus. While on earth, He was a master of prayer. In heaven, where He is seated on the right hand of the Father, His present day ministry is still intercession.

> *Wherefore he is able so save them to the uttermost that come unto God by him, seeing he ever liveth to make intercession for them.*   *Hebrews 7:25*

To examine Jesus' entire prayer life on earth in detail would be a insurmountable task. Instead we are going to examine only three instances in His earthly ministry where he prayed into manifestation the purposes and plans of the Father concerning Him. Jesus himself had this to say about God's purposes for Him.

> *Then said I, Lo, I come (in the volume of*
> *the book it is written of me,) to do thy will,*
> *O God.*   *Hebrews 10:7*

He was effectively saying that, in a heavenly book, God's purposes concerning Him had been written in meticulous detail. His job on earth was to do what was written in that book. Simple as it might appear, that statement from the lips of Jesus was loaded with great responsibility. For between the purposes of God and their fulfillment is a great gulf. Prayer is the effective bridge.

In the first thirty years of His life, he lived in relative anonymity in the town of Nazareth. His trade was carpentry and, in general, he lived a blameless life, obeying and fulfilling the laws and statutes in the Laws of Moses. Much as He was the Word in flesh, He must have read the Law and Prophets many times; and He had a clear picture through God's Word about the prophecies concerning Him.

Then came His baptism in the Jordan river! That was the turning point. Jesus the private man had become Jesus the public figure.

> *Now when all the people were baptized, it came to pass, that Jesus also being baptized, and praying, the heaven was opened,*
> *And the Holy Ghost descended in a bodily shape like a dove upon him, and a voice came from heaven, which said, Thou art my beloved Son, in thee I am well pleased.*
> *Luke 3:21-22*

It is important to realize that the heavens did not open to release the Holy Ghost upon Jesus until He prayed after the baptism:

> *... and praying, the heaven was opened...* *Luke 3:21*

An important principle we have to under-stand here is that the frontiers of heaven open as a response to prayer. If you want to permanently open heaven over your life, then you have to be a man or woman of prayer. As I stated earlier, we are going to examine three examples, among of many, where

Jesus prayed through the promises and purposes of God.

Begin the Mission

Right after His baptism and the descent of the Holy Ghost upon Him, Jesus was ready to start the three year ministry that would ultimately lead to Golgotha. However, much as He knew that the time was ripe, he made no move. Instead, He made a strategic journey into the wilderness.

And Jesus being full of the Holy Ghost returned from Jordan, and was led by the Spirit into the wilderness. **Luke 4:1**

The scene was set for an epic battle in the spirit. From the fall of Adam, Satan had enjoyed a field day in the earth. Though, he had failed to locate and abort Jesus' coming to earth, he still had a tremendous war machine in place to oppose the purposes of God concerning Jesus' earthly ministry. This fact was not lost on Jesus. He knew that before the cross, when Satan would be dealt a knock-out punch, He had to contend with Him in spiritual warfare.

For forty days and nights, Jesus progressively weakened Satan's grip over mankind. In night after night of intense bombardment, He was serving notice to principalities, right down the command structure to demon spirits, that a new order was coming. He made it abundantly clear that He had the fire power to do them severe damage. He was not going to back down and go away. What was written in the volume of the books had to come to pass.

Satan was in absolute panic. Jesus was his worst nightmare. With each passing day, Satan witnessed the beating that his forces were taking under this man in the wilderness. Every counter-attack he tried had failed, as this troublesome Messiah located his every move through the gifts of the Spirit.

After forty days of non-stop bombardment, Jesus knew that He had dislodged and weakened the forces of evil. That is when Satan decided to pay the man a visit in the wilderness. Three times he tried to tempt Jesus; and on all occasions, Jesus used the Word of God to ward him off. Satan had to leave for a season to lick his wounds. Jesus, on the other hand, was blazing with Holy Ghost fire—ready for action.

There are important lessons to be learned from what Jesus did in the wilderness. He had a blueprint from God about His ministry, yet He had to pray and fast to secure it in the spirit. He did not just go ahead and start fulfilling the blueprint. Too often, we rush to try and fulfill a prophecy instead of first praying through to secure it in the spirit. Remember! You receive the prophecy, pray it through, <u>and then act</u>.

> ***And Jesus returned in the power of the Spirit into Galilee...   Luke 4:14***

It is important to grasp the fact that He was ***led by the Spirit*** into the wilderness, but returned after forty days ***in the power of the Spirit***. <u>It is one thing to be led by the Spirit and a totally different thing to walk in the power of the Spirit.</u> Prayer and fasting bridge the gap.

Decision Time

After His return from the wilderness, Jesus began His ministry in earnest. Never before had the Jews witnessed such a spectacle. The blind were seeing, the deaf were hearing, and the lame were walking. The words that emanated from His lips did something unique.

> ***And they were astonished at his doctrine: for his word was power.   Luke 4:32***

In the midst of all the success, Jesus knew that success without a successor breeds failure. A time would come when He would have to go to the cross, die, resurrect, and ascend into heaven. Who were the ones who were going to continue the work?

Out of the many disciples that followed Him, who were the ones that He was going to train to expand the work? By the prompting of the Spirit, He knew that He had to make a decision on the matter early in His ministry. What He did not want to do was to use His five senses to make a decision. He had to pray into manifestation the selection dealing with this matter written in the volume of the book.

> *And it came to pass in those days, that he went out into a mountain to pray, and continued all night in prayer to God.*
>
> *And when it was day, he called unto him his disciples: and of them chose twelve, who also he named apostles.*　　*Luke 6:12-13*

How interesting! The Bible states that Jesus had to pray all night in order to receive from God the list of the twelve who he would specially train to continue the work. Imagine what would have happened if He had not prayed and gone on to make a decision by the flesh. Many a time when we have to make a decision, we do so based on the things we see instead of praying until we get clearance from the Spirit. In this instance, Jesus didn't pray for five minutes and then walk out. He had to travail until the answer came, and He had the release.

Crisis Time

Ever sine the trip to Caesarea Philippi where Peter through the Holy Ghost had said: *"Thou art the Christ, the Son the living God"* (Matthew 16:16), Jesus had begun to speak more often about His coming death. These were not the most pleasant of days for Him. He would have to face the cross if mankind was to be redeemed from sin and the demands of a righteous God met. Shortly after, the Father sent Him a reminder that His death was not too far away.

...he took Peter and John and James, and went up into a mountain to pray.

And as he prayed, the fashion of his countenance was altered, and his raiment was white and glistening.

And, behold there talked with him two men, which were Moses and Elias:

Who appeared in glory, and spoke of his decease which he should accomplish at Jerusalem.   *Luke 9:28-31*

The Father, after Jesus had prayed, caused Moses and Elijah to appear in glory with a message—He would die in Jerusalem. Always before Jesus was the powerful prophecy given by Isaiah hundreds of years before:

He was despised and rejected of men; a man of sorrows, and acquainted with grief; and we hid as it were our faces from him; he was despised, and we esteemed him not.

Surely he hath borne our briefs, and carried our sorrows: yet we did esteem him stricken, smitten of God, and afflicted.

But he was wounded for our transgressions, he was bruised for our iniquity: the chastisement for our peace was upon him; and with his stripes we are healed.

Isaiah 53:3-5

The prophecy was clear about the fact that the torture before Jesus' execution was going to be gruesome. In addition, Jesus would be rejected of men. He would be filled with grief and much sorrow.

The day of the Passover arrived and after the last supper, Jesus went with His disciples to Gethsemane. Asking His disciples to sit down, He took Peter,

James, and John further inside and told them what was in His heart.

My soul is exceeding sorrowful unto death: tarry ye here and watch. Mark 14:34

Here was where the rubber met the road. Jesus knew that in the next few hours the prophecies of His death would have to come to pass. We see tremendous pressure on His soul.

And he was withdrawn from them about a stone's cast, and kneeled down, and prayed.
   Saying, Father if thou be willing, remove this cup from me: nevertheless not my will, but thine, be done.
   And there appeared an angel unto him from heaven strengthening him.
   And being in agony he prayed more earnestly: and his sweat was as it were great drops of blood falling down to the ground.
                              Luke 22:41-44

As Jesus began to pray, your and my fate hung in the balance. His soul did not at all relish the suffering of the cross or the separation from the Father that He would experience after taking on the sin of the world. We see Jesus' humanity, as He seems to monetarily crack under the pressure, asking the Father if it is possible to offer an alternative to the cross. His spirit man, however, comes through impressing of God the need for His will to be done. Then Jesus begins to go into strong travail in order for His soul to line up with the purposes of God. He prays so earnestly that the globules of sweat coming from his body are likened to great drops of blood. He finally breaks through in prayer and has a release to proceed to Calvary. Humanity is saved.

I personally believe that if Jesus had not prayed through the purposes of God pertaining to the cross, He would have gone ahead in obedience; but He might not have had the physical strength and enablement to overcome the torture and trial and then proceed on to Calvary. Remember that He is our example. If He was required to pray for the will of God to come to pass in His life, then we can do no less. We have to pray everything written about us in heaven and in the volume of the book.

Chapter Eight

Warning!

Modern Day Deception

Many times over the preceding chapters, I have pointed out the importance of praying for the manifestation of prophecy from the LORD. Even as I write this to you there is a movement spreading throughout Christendom that disturbs me greatly. Many are running to embrace the subtle satanic deception of the faith movement, believing that faith carries more weight than prayer. "All you have to do is master the art of the faith confession. All of this praying is simply betraying your lack of faith," is the cry of many modern day teachers. Please do not give heed to these seducing spirits!

This is merely a plot of the enemy to undermine the strength of the church.

The Scriptures clearly state, ...*" the effectual fervent prayer of the righteous man avails much,"* (James 5:16), *not* the faith of the righteous. Some get stuck on the point that, *"without faith it is impossible to please God,"* (Hebrews 11:6); and it is true. It is impossible to please God if we do not come to a saving knowledge of His Son Jesus. It is our belief, of faith, that Jesus Christ is the Son of God who died for our sins that compels us to confess Him as Lord by submitting our lives to God in prayer. Without the confession of faith through prayer, our faith is worthless.

The Bible states that, *"the devils also believe and tremble."* (James 2:19). However, their belief will not be enough to gain them entry into heaven at the last day.

When we establish a relationship with God through Jesus, we become couriers of God's authority in the earth realm. Satan is well aware of who is backed up with heavenly authority credentials and who is not. Remember the story of the two brothers of Sceva?

Then certain of vagabond Jew, exorcists, took upon them to call over them which had evil spirits the name of the Lord Jesus, saying, We adjure you by Jesus whom Paul preacheth.

And there were seven sons of Sceva, a Jew, and chief of the priests, which did so.

And the evil spirit answered and said, Jesus I know and Paul I know, but who are ye?

And the man in whom the evil spirit was leaped on them, and overcame them, and prevailed against them, so that they fled out of that house naked and wounded.

Acts 19:13-16

Obviously these men had the faith that all it took to overcome those oppressed was the name of Jesus. After all, they had witnessed Paul and the other apostles using this simple formula. They had faith, but Satan knew they did not have the right relationship. He knew they had no accreditation from God to exercise authority over them.

Relationships are established and maintained through communication. Prayer is communication with God. Only through communication with Him, can we receive His wisdom for living a victorious life and His instructions for birthing His purposes into the midst.

The Work of Faith

Jesus crucified the flesh, built up His spirit man, and received instructions daily from His Heavenly Father. He was a man of great faith, yet He understood that **"faith without works is dead**." Prayer is faith in motion. It calls the universe to order, and subjects it to the obedience of what God has written and declared. Prayer is the work of faith.

Faith and prayer must go hand in hand. Those who embrace the "name it, claim it, and frame it" mentality are simply casting off the responsibility of living the disciplined life of a true joint heir with Christ. They will eventually awaken from a fleshly stupor to find themselves spiritually bankrupt with no oil in their lamps. These are the ones who fall away in the face of trials and storms.

It is the faith that God is behind you that equips you with the assurance you need to say to the mountain, "Be thou removed." It is prayer that removes the mountain. To believe that it is faith alone that removes the mountain, to believe that it is by faith alone that things are accomplished, is an arrogant stance that removes God from His sovereign position.

God is well able to do as He pleases without your faith, but He relies on the prayers of the saints to activate heaven into accomplishing His purposes on earth. As you read thorough the Bible, repeatedly you will see where God stirred up someone to pray. Then things begin to happen! The moves of God never preceded the prayers, and things did not happen merely because people believed the promise. *Amen!*

The Spirit-Led Life

Remember, in the beginning was the Word, then the Word became flesh. First, there was God's purpose; then we were formed to fulfill that purpose. The Word will always precede the manifestation of God's movements. Prayer is the call that propels the Word into activation. God needs us to pray! Why?—because He has established a rule in the universe that His agenda in the earth realm must be carried out by human vessels.

Human beings are the legal way of entry into the earth realm for God's spirit to operate now that the earth is under the domain of Satan. Satan also requires the use of human vessels to carry out his agenda—thus the constant attack and tempting of our flesh. The flesh must be crucified through fasting in order to give way to the spirit of God taking predominance in our lives. *Lord Jesus Amen!*

It is spirit-controlled living that paves the way for God's Word and purpose to be performed in the earth. Jesus knew that a spirit-led life was crucial to victorious living. This is why He took the time to teach the disciples to pray. After teaching them the basics, he further instructed them, *"When you fast... When you pray... ."* Notice, He did not say, *"If."* These were not options in His book. He even went further to teach them that some deliverances would not be accomplished without fasting.

> ***Howbeit this kind goeth not out but by prayer and fasting.   Matthew 17: 21***

This is War

You must remember that you are in a war. Believing the battle has been won is not enough. We must exercise strong-arm tactics in the spirit in order to secure God's purposes in our lives. Satan will contend with one's faith, but flee from the prayer of a submitted saint. You must vow to do more that just believe, you must get violent in the spirit over God's promises for your life. Jesus said, ***"The kingdom of heaven suffereth violence, and the violent take it by force."*** (Matthew 11:12). Paul, also a great man of faith, was not in a state of denial when it came to the necessity of warfare:

For we wrestle not against flesh and blood, but against principalities, against powers, against the rulers of darkness of this world, against spiritual wickedness in high places.

Wherefore take unto you the whole armour of God, that ye may be able to withstand in the evil day, and having done all, to stand.

Stand therefore, having your loins girt about with truth, and having on the breastplate of righteousness;

And your feet shod with the preparation of the gospel of peace;

Above all, taking the shield of faith, wherewith ye shall be able to quench all the fiery darts of the wicked.

And take the helmet of salvation, and the sword of the Spirit, which is the word of God:

Praying always with all power and supplication in the Spirit and watching thereunto with all perseverance and supplication for all saints.   Ephesians 6: 12-18

> *Paul makes it clear that more than faith is required in order to triumph over the enemy. Only after having done all are we instructed to stand and assume a position of waiting for God's intervention. What does "all" include? The Word of the Lord sums it up nicely:*
>
> *If my people, which are called by my name shall humble themselves, and pray, and seek my face, and turn from their wicked ways; then will I hear from heaven, and will forgive their sin, and will heal their land.*
>
> *2 Chronicles 7:14*

Again, faith does not claim the spotlight here. Instead the Word of God gives a long list of responsibilities that most of us do not like to address. Yet there is no way around these directions if we truly desire to see God's purposes come to pass in our lives. This does not apply just to, say, a war-torn country, but to every situation in your life, whatever you may desire from God. Prayer is essential. It is the lifeblood of the believer. Even as Jesus hung on the cross dying; He prayed. And He is not finished! The Bible tells us that He ever lives to make intercession for us (Hebrews 7:25). Jesus is still praying.

How much more should we apply our selves to be diligent in prayer?

> *Men ought always to pray, and not to faint.* *Luke 18: 1*

It is my prayer that this book will give you greater revelation of the power you have through prayer to accomplish two very important tasks: taking hold of the promises of God for your lives and destroying the plots of the enemy to hinder our Heavenly Father's purposes from being performed. I encourage you to remember who you are in Christ and the power you have been given because of His shed blood at Calvary.

> *But as many as received him, to them gave he power to become the sons of God. Even to them that believe on his name:* *John 1:12*

Stand fast in your faith and be determined to put the enemy in his rightful place. Remember, you have been given the keys to the kingdom.

> *And I will give unto thee the keys of the kingdom of heaven: and whatsoever*

thou shalt bind on earth shall be bound in heaven: and whatsoever thou shalt loose on earth shall be loosed in heaven.

Matthew 16:19

This means God Himself has proclaimed that you have been given the power to allow or disallow the movement of the enemy in your life. Decide to utilize your God-given authority to possess all that God has in store for you. Begin today to pray and wage an intelligent warfare on behalf of yourself and your loved ones. Expect the heavens to be moved and the weapons the enemy has forged against you to be destroyed. Remember, your commitment to prayer is the key to seeing the purposes of God to fulfillment in your life.

WARFARE PRAYER

Father, in the name of Jesus, I superimpose your prophetic purposes concerning my life over and against all demonic and satanic activists. I bring down every manifestation, operation, manipulation, resistance, limitation, exploitation, set-back, disappointment, spell, unscriptural prayer and desire, every demonic and satanic demand and claim upon my life. Furthermore, I uproot and destroy any assignment of the enemy whatsoever to hinder your prophetic purposes for me in the name of Jesus.

I superimpose the prophetic purposes of God over the fear of the unknown, over the walls of opposition and resistance, and over satanic and demonic predications and projections in the name of Jesus.

I plead the blood of Jesus against persons without bodies assigned to frustrate, hinder, and to disorganize me in any shape or form in the name of Jesus. I plead the blood of Jesus against them, and by the blood, I nullify, I overrule, I cancel, I revoke and reverse any death wish, and all of their decisions against me. By the blood of Jesus, I halt any accusing finger. I silence the voice of the accuser in the name of Jesus, the Son of the Living God.

Amen